Table of Contents

Preface

This book is a guide, but if it were a novel, here's how it would start:

Once upon a time, in the ceaseless tumult of the financial markets, there was a young man named Julien. Each day, Julien would rise before dawn, armed with courage and hope, to face the unpredictable ocean of figures and curves on his computer. With a mix of enthusiasm and trepidation, he drew trend lines, deciphered economic indicators, and plumbed the depths of financial news. Yet, despite his efforts and perseverance, Julien often found himself at a loss in the face of his task. The market, like a capricious giant, seemed to toy with his emotions and savings.

One evening, as the last light of twilight drowned in the horizon, Julien, exhausted, contemplated the recent losses that sprawled across his screen, like a battlefield after the war. It was in these moments of solitude that the weight of a trader's loneliness felt most cruelly. "If only," he murmured, "if only I had a guide, a mentor, something or someone to illuminate my path through this labyrinthine market."

It is here that our story takes a less ordinary path, that of artificial intelligence. Imagine a world where Julien, our Julien, could rely on a companion not of flesh and bone, but of bits and artificial neurons. A silent ally, always present, who analyzes, calculates, and proposes with unparalleled precision and speed. This world is no longer entirely a dream.

This book that you hold in your hands, dear readers, is the beacon in the storm, the compass for every modern-day Julien. "Artificial Intelligence for Everyday Traders" is not just a collection of tips and strategies; it is an open door to a new era where artificial intelligence becomes an indispensable trading partner, transforming challenges into opportunities, uncertainties into predictions.

Through these pages, we will explore how tools once reserved for engineers and mathematicians are now accessible to everyone. With simplicity and elegance, we will unveil the mysteries of these technologies, so that no trader ever feels alone in front of their screen again.

Let yourself be guided on this adventure where tradition meets innovation, and where Julien, perhaps, will finally find the path to success. Because, after all, navigating the world of trading with artificial intelligence is not just a matter of logic or profit; it is an art, and like all art, it requires inspiration and, yes, a little magic.

Introduction

Imagine this: You're glued to your screen, frantically refreshing stock quotes, frantically refreshing stock quotes, emotions swinging wildly with every market tick.
Fear whispers "Sell!" while greed screams "Hold on!"

Sound familiar?

Millions of everyday traders face this very dilemma. But what if there was a weapon in your arsenal that could cut through the noise and help you make data-driven decisions? Enter Artificial Intelligence (AI). This book will show you exactly how to leverage AI to transform your trading strategy and level the playing field, even against seasoned professionals.

Imagine a trading world where the difference between profit and loss is not just intuition, but an advanced intelligence capable of analyzing millions of data points in the blink of an eye.

According to a groundbreaking analysis by the Financial Markets Technology Research Center, AI-powered trading algorithms have demonstrated the potential to outstrip traditional trading strategies by an astonishing 73%. Shocked? You're not alone.

'Artificial Intelligence for Everyday Traders: How to Utilize AI in Your Trading Strategy' is your essential guide to navigating this new terrain.
Whether you're a novice trader or have years of experience, this book will unlock the secrets of using AI to uncover market trends, automate complex trading decisions, and ultimately, elevate your trading performance to new heights.

Join us on this transformative journey and discover how to leverage the unprecedented power of artificial intelligence in your trading strategy."

Chapter 1: Introduction to Artificial Intelligence in Trading

The Basics of Artificial Intelligence

In today's fast-paced and ever-evolving trading landscape, understanding the basics of artificial intelligence (AI) is crucial for non-professional traders looking to stay ahead of the curve. AI has revolutionized the way trading is conducted, providing traders with powerful tools and insights to make more informed decisions and optimize their trading strategies.

Ray Dalio, the founder of Bridgewater Associates, one of the world's largest hedge funds, about the use of AI in trading is telling :

"I believe that the use of artificial intelligence in trading is here to stay and will continue to revolutionize the industry. AI has the potential to analyze vast amounts of data in real-time, identify patterns and trends that human traders may miss, and execute trades with speed and precision. As technology continues to advance, AI algorithms will play an increasingly important role in shaping the future of financial markets." - Ray Dalio

Ray Dalio's insights on the use of AI in trading highlight the transformative impact that artificial intelligence and sophisticated algorithms are having on the financial industry.

At its core, AI refers to the simulation of human intelligence processes by machines, specifically computer systems. These systems are programmed to analyze vast amounts of data, identify patterns, and make predictions based on historical data and real-time market conditions. By leveraging AI technology, non-professional traders can gain a competitive edge by accessing sophisticated algorithms that can process data at speeds far beyond human capacity.

One of the key benefits of AI in trading is its ability to automate repetitive tasks and execute trades with precision and speed. This can help traders capitalize on market opportunities in real-time, without the need for constant monitoring and manual intervention. Additionally, AI can provide traders with valuable insights and recommendations, enabling them to make more informed decisions and minimize the risks associated with emotional trading.

To effectively utilize AI in your trading strategy, it is important to have a basic understanding of how AI works and the different types of AI technologies available. Machine learning, deep learning, and natural language processing are just a few examples of AI techniques that can be used to analyze market data and generate actionable insights.

By mastering the basics of AI and incorporating AI technology into your trading strategy, non-professional traders can unlock new opportunities for profit and success in the dynamic world of trading. Stay tuned for more insights and tips on how to leverage AI in your trading journey.

Here are some things to consider before using AI for trading:

AI is a tool, not a guarantee : AI can't predict the future, and markets are inherently unpredictable. Always maintain control over your trading decisions.

Data Quality Matters : The effectiveness of AI depends on the quality of data it's trained on. Ensure your chosen platform uses reliable data sources.

Understanding is Key: While AI can identify patterns, it's crucial to understand the underlying logic behind those patterns to make informed decisions.

Start Small: If you're new to AI trading, start with a small portion of your capital and gradually increase your reliance on AI as you gain experience and confidence.

The History of AI in Trading

The evolution of artificial intelligence (AI) in trading is marked by major technological advances and key moments that have transformed the way financial markets work. Here's an overview of this evolution:

1980s: The first trading algorithms

- 1980s: The era of the first trading algorithms began with the introduction of automated systems capable of executing stock market orders. These systems, called "Program Trading", used simple algorithms to automate trades based on predefined criteria.

- 1987: "Black Monday", a global stock market crash, highlights the potential impact of automated trading and prompts increased regulation of trading systems.

1990s: The Era of Expert Systems

- 1990s: During this period, expert systems become increasingly popular in trading. These systems, which are primitive forms of artificial intelligence, use rules based on specific knowledge to make trading decisions.

VPX (Virtual Portfolio eXperience): VPX is an emblematic example of an expert system from this era. Developed by Reuters, VPX was designed to help traders manage their portfolios using predefined rules and models. It could simulate trading strategies and test different market scenarios to optimize investment decisions. Using VPX, traders could analyze the performance of their portfolios and adjust their strategies accordingly, representing a significant advance over manual methods.

VPX and other expert systems of this period marked a milestone in the evolution of the use of AI in trading.

These tools enabled traders to benefit from computer-assisted decision-making, reducing human error and improving the overall efficiency of trading strategies. Expert systems like VPX have also laid the foundations for future developments in algorithmic trading and modern AI. By automating certain tasks and providing analyses based on defined rules, they paved the way for more sophisticated algorithms and the use of machine learning techniques in the decades to follow.

- 1998: The introduction of "Regulation ATS" (Alternative Trading Systems) by the SEC (Securities and Exchange Commission) in the USA enables the development of alternative trading platforms and electronic trading systems.

2000s: The advent of high-frequency trading

- 2000s: High-frequency trading (HFT) emerges, using advanced algorithms to execute thousands of trades in a fraction of a second. This is made possible by improvements in computing power and connection speed.

- 2007: The introduction of Reg NMS (Regulation National Market System) by the SEC aims to modernize and improve the efficiency of the US market, further facilitating HFT.

2010s: Machine Learning and Modern AI

- 2010s: Machine learning techniques begin to be integrated into trading strategies. These algorithms can learn and adapt from historical data to continually improve their performance.

- 2012: The use of neural networks and deep learning is spreading, enabling more complex and accurate data analysis. For example, companies like Renaissance Technologies use these techniques to optimize their quantitative trading strategies.

2020s: AI accessible to non-professional traders

- 2020s: AI is becoming increasingly accessible to non-professional traders thanks to the development of online trading platforms incorporating AI tools. Applications such as Robinhood and eToro offer AI-based features to help users make informed trading decisions.

- 2021: The popularity of "Robo-Advisors", automated financial advisors using AI, continues to grow, democratizing access to sophisticated investment strategies for the general public.

Could the 1929 crisis have been avoided with AI?

The Great Depression and AI: A Futuristic Hypothesis

The crisis of 1929, known as the Great Depression, was a complex event resulting from multiple economic, financial and psychological factors. While it is difficult to state with certainty that artificial intelligence could have prevented such a crisis, we can speculate on some aspects where AI could potentially have made a difference.

Prediction and prevention

AI, capable of analyzing huge quantities of data in real time, could have detected warning signs such as economic imbalances and speculative bubbles. By alerting financial authorities to impending dangers earlier, preventive measures could have been taken. In addition, machine learning and deep learning algorithms could have modeled complex risk scenarios and proposed preventive interventions. For example, AI could have analyzed investor behavior and identified dangerous trends before they got out of hand.

Reaction and intervention

In the event of rapid market fluctuations, AI could have reacted faster than humans to stabilize the markets. Automated interventions, such as temporarily suspending trading in the event of extreme volatility, could have prevented drastic falls. AI could also help by governments and financial institutions adapt their economic policies in real time, by quickly adjusting interest rates or taking fiscal measures to stabilize the economy.

Education and information

AI could also play an important role in investor education by providing personalized analysis and recommendations, helping to avoid imprudent investment behavior.

Limitations and considerations

However, it is important to note that AI is not a magic solution. Even with the most advanced technologies, certain human aspects, such as panic and overconfidence, could still play a crucial role in financial crises. What's more, economic and financial policy decisions often involve political and social considerations that algorithms cannot fully capture.

In summary, while AI could probably have mitigated some of the effects of the 1929 crisis through better data analysis, early risk detection and rapid market reaction, it's hard to argue that it would have prevented the crisis altogether. Financial crises are often the result of multiple interconnected factors, including unpredictable human behavior and complex political decisions.

Concrete examples

The evolution of AI in trading is a story of rapid technological progress and financial market transformation. From the first simple algorithms to sophisticated machine learning systems, AI has enabled traders of all kinds to improve their strategies and optimize their performance. With each new advance, AI continues to redefine what's possible in the world of trading.

Here are a few examples that have already marked the history of trading with Artificial Intelligence:

- **Renaissance Technologies**: Founded in 1982 by Jim Simons, this hedge fund management company uses advanced mathematical models and algorithms for quantitative trading. Their Medallion fund is famous for its exceptional returns, attributed to their early use of AI.

- **Kensho Technologies**: Founded in 2013, this company uses AI technologies to provide advanced financial analytics. Kensho was acquired by S&P Global in 2018 for $550 million.

- **DeepMind**: In 2016, Google subsidiary DeepMind developed an AI capable of predicting stock price movements with remarkable accuracy using deep learning techniques.

The Evolution of AI in Trading

In recent years, the use of artificial intelligence (AI) in trading has become increasingly popular among non-professional traders. The evolution of AI in trading has revolutionized the way everyday traders approach the stock market, providing them with powerful tools and insights to make more informed investment decisions.

One of the key ways AI has evolved in trading is through the development of sophisticated algorithms that can analyze vast amounts of data in real-time. These algorithms are able to quickly identify patterns and trends in the market that may be missed by human traders, giving everyday traders a competitive edge. Additionally, AI can also automate the trading process, executing trades at lightning speed based on predefined criteria.

Currently a concrete application is the use of algorithmic trading by institutional investors and large financial firms to manage their portfolios more efficiently. These algorithms can analyze vast amounts of data, including historical price movements, market trends, and economic indicators, to optimize asset allocation, risk management, and trading strategies. Overall, the application of sophisticated algorithms in trading has revolutionized the financial markets by enabling traders to make faster, more informed, and data-driven decisions that can lead to better investment outcomes.

Another important development in the evolution of AI in trading is the use of machine learning techniques to improve trading strategies. Machine learning algorithms can adapt and learn from past data, continuously refining their trading strategies to maximize profits and minimize losses. This allows non-professional traders to benefit from the same advanced technology used by institutional investors.

Furthermore, AI has also made trading more accessible to non-professional traders through the development of user-friendly trading platforms and apps that incorporate AI technology. These platforms provide traders with easy-to-use tools and resources to analyze market data, track performance, and make informed decisions.

Overall, the evolution of AI in trading has opened up new opportunities for non-professional traders to enhance their trading strategies and improve their overall performance in the market. By leveraging the power of AI, everyday traders can level the playing field with institutional investors and increase their chances of success in the stock market.

Benefits of Using AI in Trading

Artificial Intelligence (AI) has revolutionized the way trading is done in today's financial markets. For non-professional traders looking to enhance their trading strategies, incorporating AI into their trading routine can offer a wide range of benefits. Here are some of the key advantages of using AI in trading:

1. Increased Efficiency: AI technology can analyze vast amounts of data at a speed and accuracy that is far beyond human capabilities. This allows traders to make quicker and more informed decisions, leading to more efficient trades.

2. Improved Decision Making: By utilizing AI algorithms, traders can access advanced analytical tools that can identify patterns and trends in the market. This can help traders make more accurate predictions and optimize their trading strategies.

3. Reduced Emotional Bias: One of the biggest challenges for non-professional traders is managing emotions such as fear and greed, which can lead to impulsive or irrational trading decisions. AI systems operate based on algorithms and logic, removing emotional bias from the trading process.

4. Risk Management: AI can help traders better manage risk by providing real-time analysis of market conditions and potential threats to their positions. This can help traders minimize losses and protect their investments.

5. Diversification: AI tools can analyze a wide range of assets and markets simultaneously, allowing traders to diversify their portfolios more effectively. This can help spread risk and maximize potential returns.

According to a report by research firm MarketsandMarkets, the global AI in the financial market is projected to reach $26.67 billion by 2027, growing at a CAGR of 23.37% from 2020. This significant growth can be attributed to the increasing adoption of AI technologies, including machine learning, natural language processing, and deep learning, in trading and investment activities.

Furthermore, a study by the World Economic Forum estimated that AI-driven hedge funds outperformed their human-managed counterparts by 4% to 6% per year on average. This outperformance is attributed to AI's ability to analyze vast amounts of data, identify patterns, and execute trades faster and more efficiently than human traders.

Overall, the impact of AI in trading is substantial, with AI-powered algorithms and technologies revolutionizing the way financial markets operate and providing traders with powerful tools to make informed decisions and optimize investment strategies.

In conclusion, incorporating AI into your trading strategy can offer a range of benefits that can help non-professional traders improve their overall performance. By leveraging the power of AI technology, traders can enhance their decision-making process, reduce emotional bias, and maximize their trading efficiency.

If you are still not convinced, here is one example of an individual trader who publicly advocates for the use of artificial intelligence (AI) in trading is Andrew Ng, a prominent figure in the AI and technology industry. Andrew Ng is a computer scientist, entrepreneur, and co-founder of Google Brain, who has been vocal about the potential of AI in trading.

In a Forbes interview, Andrew Ng emphasized the importance of AI in finance and trading, stating that AI algorithms can analyze vast amounts of data, identify patterns, and make informed trading decisions faster and more efficiently than human traders. He highlighted the potential for AI to revolutionize the financial industry and improve trading outcomes for individual investors.

While there may not be as many well-known individual traders publicly discussing their use of AI in trading, there is a growing trend of retail traders and investors incorporating AI-powered tools and platforms into their trading strategies. These tools can provide valuable insights, automate trading processes, and help individual traders make more informed decisions in the complex and dynamic financial markets.

Chapter 2:
Understanding AI Trading Strategies

Machine Learning Algorithms for Trading

Machine learning algorithms have revolutionized the way traders approach the financial markets. These sophisticated algorithms can analyze vast amounts of data and identify patterns that are difficult, if not impossible, for humans to detect. In this subchapter, we will explore some of the most commonly used machine learning algorithms in trading and how non-professional traders can leverage them to improve their trading strategies.

One popular machine learning algorithm used in trading is the random forest algorithm. This algorithm works by creating multiple decision trees and combining their predictions to make more accurate forecasts. Random forests are particularly effective in handling large datasets and complex market conditions, making them a valuable tool for non-professional traders looking to enhance their trading strategies.

Another widely used machine learning algorithm in trading is the support vector machine (SVM). SVMs are used for classification and regression tasks, making them ideal for predicting market trends and identifying potential trading opportunities. By utilizing SVMs, non-professional traders can make more informed decisions based on the patterns and trends identified by the algorithm.

Gradient boosting is another powerful machine learning algorithm that is commonly used in trading. This algorithm works by combining multiple weak learners to create a strong predictive model. Gradient boosting is particularly effective in handling noisy data and non-linear relationships, making it a valuable tool for non-professional traders looking to improve their trading strategies.

In conclusion, machine learning algorithms offer non-professional traders a powerful tool to enhance their trading strategies and make more informed decisions in the financial markets. By leveraging algorithms such as random forests, SVMs, and gradient boosting, traders can gain a competitive edge and increase their chances of success in the ever-evolving world of trading with AI.

Practical use of Machine Learning Algorithms by Amateur Traders

Amateur traders can exploit algorithms such as random forests, SVMs and gradient boosting to improve their trading strategies by following a few key steps.

Random Forests

1. **Data Collection**: Gather historical data on stock prices, trading volumes and other financial indicators.
2. **Data Preparation**: Clean and pre-process data so that it is usable by the algorithm. This includes handling missing values and normalizing variables.
3. **Algorithm training**: Use machine learning software (such as Scikit-learn in Python) to train the random forest algorithm on your data.
4. **Predictions**: Use the trained model to predict future stock price trends and make trading decisions based on these predictions.

Support Vector Machines (SVM)

1. **Feature Definition**: Identify relevant features for classification or regression, such as technical indicators (RSI, MACD) and trading volumes.
2. **Model Training**: Use software like Scikit-learn to train the SVM with your historical data.
3. **Classification and Predictions**: The SVM model can be used to classify market movements (up or down) or to predict future prices, helping to identify trading opportunities.

Gradient Boosting

1. **Data Aggregation**: Combine different data sources, including stock prices, economic news and sentiment indicators.
2. **Progressive training**: Use tools like XGBoost to train the gradient boosting model on your data. This process optimizes predictions by combining several weak models.
3. **Analysis and Predictions**: The resulting model can handle noisy data and non-linear relationships, providing robust forecasts for trading decisions.

Tools and resources

To put these techniques into practice, amateur traders can use machine learning platforms and libraries such as:

- **Python**: With libraries such as **Scikit-learn, TensorFlow** and **XGBoost.**
- **R**: With packages such as **caret** and **randomForest**.
- **Trading software**: Some software packages offer built-in AI and machine learning capabilities.

By integrating these algorithms into their trading routines, amateur traders can take advantage of advanced AI capabilities to analyze data, reduce emotional biases and improve their investment decisions.

Neural Networks in Trading

Neural networks have revolutionized the way trading is done in the financial markets. These advanced AI algorithms are designed to mimic the way the human brain works, making them incredibly effective at analyzing complex patterns in market data. For non-professional traders looking to take their trading strategy to the next level, understanding how neural networks can be utilized in trading is essential.

One of the key benefits of using neural networks in trading is their ability to process vast amounts of data at lightning speed. This means that they can quickly analyze market trends and make predictions based on historical data, helping traders make more informed decisions. Neural networks can also adapt to changing market conditions, making them particularly useful in volatile markets.

Another advantage of neural networks is their ability to learn from past mistakes and continuously improve their predictions. This means that over time, the accuracy of their predictions can increase, leading to more profitable trades. For non-professional traders who may not have the time or expertise to conduct in-depth market analysis, neural networks can provide a valuable shortcut to making better trading decisions.

However, it's important to note that while neural networks can be powerful tools in trading, they are not foolproof. It's essential for non-professional traders to understand the limitations of neural networks and not rely solely on them for making trading decisions. Instead, neural networks should be used in conjunction with other tools and strategies to create a well-rounded trading strategy.

Exploiting Neural Networks by Amateur Traders: A Practical Example

This example illustrates how a trader might use neural networks for educational purposes. In reality, the use of neural networks is undoubtedly more complex. But this should get you started.

Step 1: Data collection

An amateur trader starts by collecting historical data on stock prices, trading volumes and other financial indicators. This data can be obtained from trading platforms or financial APIs.

Step 2: Data preparation

Data must be cleaned and prepared. This includes handling missing values, normalizing data, and creating training and test datasets.

Step 3: Neural Network Training

The trader uses software such as **TensorFlow** or **Keras** to create and train a neural network. The model is trained on the training dataset to identify patterns and trends in the historical data.

Step 4: Validation and evaluation

The model is then tested on the test dataset to assess its accuracy. Adjustments are made to optimize model performance.

Step 5: Predictions and trading decisions

Once the model has been optimized, the trader can use it to make predictions about future stock price movements. For example, if the model predicts an increase in the price of a stock, the trader may decide to buy that stock. Conversely, if the model predicts a fall, the trader may decide to sell or avoid buying.

Concrete example

Suppose an amateur trader wants to predict the price movements of Tesla shares. Here's how he might use a neural network:

1. Data Collection: The trader retrieves Tesla's historical data, including daily prices, trading volumes, and technical indicators such as the RSI (Relative Strength Index) and MACD (Moving Average Convergence Divergence).
2. Data preparation : Data are cleaned to remove missing values and normalized to ensure that all variables are on the same scale.
3. Model training: a neural network is designed and trained using **TensorFlow**. The model learns from Tesla's historical data to identify patterns that precede price increases and decreases.
4. Validation: The model is tested on an unseen dataset to assess its ability to predict future movements. Model hyperparameters, such as the number of layers and neurons, are adjusted to improve accuracy.
5. Predictions : Once satisfied with the model's performance, the trader uses it to make daily predictions on Tesla share movements. For example, if the model predicts a price increase for the following day, the trader can buy Tesla shares in anticipation of this rise.
6. Trading decisions: The trader continues to monitor the model's predictions and adjusts his positions according to the neural network's advice. Trading decisions are also cross-referenced with other analyses for a well-balanced strategy.

In conclusion, neural networks have the potential to significantly enhance the trading experience for non-professional traders. By understanding how neural networks work and how they can be integrated into a trading strategy, non-professional traders can take their trading to the next level and increase their chances of success in the financial markets.

Natural Language Processing for Trading

Natural Language Processing (NLP) is a powerful tool that can be harnessed by non-professional traders to enhance their trading strategies. By utilizing NLP in trading, everyday traders can gain valuable insights from textual data such as news articles, social media posts, and analyst reports.

NLP technology allows traders to analyze and interpret large volumes of unstructured data in real-time, helping them to make more informed decisions. By extracting key information and sentiment from textual data, traders can identify market trends, predict price movements, and assess the overall market sentiment. This can give traders a competitive edge in the fast-paced and ever-changing world of trading.

One key application of NLP in trading is sentiment analysis, which involves analyzing the sentiment expressed in news articles, social media posts, and other sources of textual data. By understanding the sentiment of market participants, traders can gauge the market's mood and make more accurate predictions about future price movements.

Another application of NLP in trading is event detection, which involves identifying and tracking events that could impact the financial markets. By monitoring news articles and social media posts for mentions of specific events, traders can stay ahead of the curve and adjust their trading strategies accordingly.

Overall, NLP can be a valuable tool for non-professional traders looking to leverage AI in their trading strategies. By harnessing the power of NLP technology, traders can gain valuable insights from textual data, improve their decision-making process, and ultimately increase their chances of success in the competitive world of trading.

As ChatGPT use NLP, we will describe more about how to use ChatGPT for your trading in another chapter.

Chapter 3:
Implementing AI in Your Trading Strategy

Selecting the Right AI Tools for Your Trading Style

As a non-professional trader looking to incorporate AI into your trading strategy, it is essential to choose the right AI tools that align with your trading style. With the plethora of AI tools available in the market, it can be overwhelming to decide which ones are best suited for your needs. In this subchapter, we will discuss some key considerations to keep in mind when selecting AI tools for your trading style.

Here are a few examples of AI tools that can be used by non-professional traders to enhance their trading experience:

- **Trade Ideas :** Trade Ideas is a market scanning tool that uses AI algorithms to identify potential trading opportunities based on criteria set by the user. It provides real-time market data, alerts, and customizable filters to help traders make informed decisions.

- **QuantConnect :** QuantConnect is a platform that allows traders to create, backtest, and deploy algorithmic trading strategies using AI and machine learning. It offers a user-friendly interface and access to a library of pre-built algorithms for traders of all skill levels.

- **Sentient Trader :** Sentient Trader is a predictive analytics tool that uses AI to analyze market cycles and trends. It helps traders identify potential turning points in the market and make more accurate predictions about future price movements.

- **Robinhood AI Trading :** Robinhood offers AI-powered trading features that provide personalized investment recommendations based on user preferences and risk tolerance. It also offers market data and trend analysis tools to help traders make informed decisions.

- **ZuluTrade :** ZuluTrade is a social trading platform that allows users to follow and copy the trading strategies of experienced traders. It uses AI algorithms to rank and filter traders based on their performance, making it easier for non-professionals to find successful trading strategies to follow.

These AI tools are designed to simplify the trading process and provide non-professional traders with access to sophisticated analysis and decision-making capabilities. However, it is important to conduct thorough research and understand how each tool works before incorporating them into your trading strategy.

The first step in selecting the right AI tools is to understand your trading style. Are you a day trader, swing trader, or long-term investor? Do you prefer technical analysis or fundamental analysis? By identifying your trading style, you can narrow down the options and focus on AI tools that are specifically designed for your type of trading.

Next, consider the features and capabilities of the AI tools. Look for tools that offer predictive analytics, trend analysis, and pattern recognition. These features can help you make informed trading decisions based on data-driven insights. Additionally, consider the level of automation offered by the AI tools. Some tools provide fully automated trading strategies, while others offer semi-automated or manual trading options. Choose a tool that aligns with your comfort level and trading experience.

Another important factor to consider is the level of customization and flexibility offered by the AI tools. Look for tools that allow you to tailor the algorithms and parameters to suit your unique trading style and preferences. This customization can help you optimize the performance of the AI tools and enhance your trading results.

In conclusion, selecting the right AI tools for your trading style requires careful consideration of your trading preferences, the features of the tools, and the level of customization available. By choosing AI tools that align with your trading style, you can effectively leverage the power of AI in your trading strategy and improve your overall trading performance.

Now let's Focus on some of them...

Trade ideas

First you have to know that Trade Ideas can refer to two things in the world of finance:

1. Trade Ideas, the company: This is an industry-owned utility that facilitates the exchange of trade ideas between institutional investors like hedge funds, banks, and asset managers [Trade Ideas - Home]. They provide a platform called the Trade Ideas Hub that connects different parties without requiring them to use the same software.

2. Trade Ideas, the software: There is also a software product called Trade Ideas that offers AI-powered stock scanning, charting, and trade alerts for personal investors [Trade Ideas: AI-Driven Stock Scanning & Charting Platform].
This software uses AI to analyze market data and identify potential trading opportunities based on technical analysis and other factors.

Here's a breakdown of each to help you understand them better:
Trade Ideas (company): is not directly relevant to everyday traders. They provide infrastructure for institutions to share trade ideas, not a product for personal investing.
Trade Ideas (software): This software uses AI for stock analysis and can be a potential tool for personal investors. It offers features like: AI-powered stock scanning to identify

potential trades Real-time charting and analysis tools Automated trade alerts based on AI analysis Backtesting capabilities to test trading strategies

Holly AI is the Virtual Trade Assistant from Trade Ideas:

Function:

- Holly AI is an AI-powered stock recommendation tool designed for premium subscribers of Trade Ideas.

- It provides real-time suggestions for stock trades, including entry and exit points.

- Holly AI focuses on intraday trading, meaning positions are typically closed out by the end of the trading day.

How it Works:

- Holly AI utilizes a set of over 60 algorithms to analyze historical market data and identify potential trading opportunities.

- These algorithms are not user-customizable and focus on technical analysis strategies.

- Holly AI scans the market each night and backtests its algorithms to generate trade ideas for the following day.

Benefits:

- Saves time by automatically scanning for potential trades.

- Provides unemotional analysis based on historical data.

- Offers clear entry and exit signals for each trade suggestion.

Limitations:

- Relies on past data, which may not always predict future performance.

- Not customizable, so users can't adjust the trading strategy behind the recommendations.

- Only available to premium subscribers of Trade Ideas.

- Focuses on intraday trading, which may not suit all investor goals.

To conclude :

Trading with AI

Holly AI can be a helpful tool for day traders or those interested in exploring AI-assisted trading. However, it's important to understand its limitations and use it alongside your own research and risk management strategies.

Here are some additional resources you might find helpful:

Trade Ideas Holly AI User Guide:

https://www.trade-ideas.com/guide/chapter/19_16/19.16Holly_AI_Auto_Trading.html

Then you have the Trade Ideas' Smart Risk AI" that refers to a set of features within their platform that utilize artificial intelligence to help users manage risk in their trades. Here's what it offers:

- ☑ AI-powered stop-loss and profit target suggestions: Trade Ideas analyzes historical data, volatility, and recent price movements to suggest appropriate stop-loss and profit target levels for each trade. These are displayed as lines on the charts and are not user-customizable.

- ☑ Smart Risk Levels: This feature highlights zones on the chart where the stock price might encounter resistance or support based on historical data and volatility. This can help traders identify potential entry and exit points that consider risk tolerance.

- ☑ Risk-to-reward ratio calculation: Trade Ideas calculates the potential risk-to-reward ratio for each trade based on the suggested stop-loss and profit target levels. This helps traders assess the potential payoff compared to the potential loss for each trade.

Trade Ideas' Smart Risk AI is a valuable tool for traders who want to incorporate AI-powered risk management into their strategy. However, it's important to remember that it's just one piece of the puzzle. Always conduct your own research, understand the limitations of AI, and maintain control over your trading decisions.

Here are some additional resources you might find helpful:

Trade Ideas Smart Risk Levels User Guide:
https://www.trade-ideas.com/guide/chapter/14_10/14.10Smart_Risk_Levels.html

Trade Ideas has received a lot of positive feedback from its users. Customers praise the platform for its impact on their trading activities, highlighting its helpfulness for beginners in the stock market, providing retail traders with an edge, and its exceptional customer service. One user mentioned a significant improvement in their trading performance after joining the TI Trading Room, while another reported a 25% gain from their first options trade based on the platform's insights.

For more detailed testimonials, you can visit Trade Ideas' website : *https://www.trade-ideas.com/*

Important Notes: While Trade Ideas (software) might be a helpful tool, it's crucial to do your own research before using any AI-powered trading platform. Remember, AI is a tool to assist your trading decisions, not a guarantee of success. Always maintain control and understand the reasoning behind the AI's suggestions.

QuantConnect (Algorithmic Trading)

QuantConnect is an open-source, cloud-based **algorithmic trading** platform designed for stocks, futures, options, cryptocurrencies and other derivatives. It is aimed at a range of users, from beginners to experienced algorithmic traders.

QuantConnect lets you design and code your own algorithmic trading strategies using Python or C#. It also supports other languages thanks to its open-source project, the Lean Algorithmic Trading Engine (LEAN), which provides a solid foundation for algorithmic development. This enables users to tailor their trading strategies to their specific needs.

In addition, QuantConnect offers cloud-based backtesting capabilities. This means that users can test their trading strategies on historical data without the need for their own IT infrastructure. This feature enables the performance of strategies to be evaluated before they are deployed with real capital, which is essential for refining and optimizing algorithms.

Once the trading strategy has been optimized through backtesting, QuantConnect enables it to be deployed live with various integrated brokers. This offers a seamless transition from development to execution, facilitating the application of strategies in the real market.

QuantConnect offers many advantages. Being open-source and free, it is accessible to a wide range of users, including those new to algorithmic trading. The cloud-based platform eliminates the need to manage one's own IT infrastructure for backtesting or live trading. What's more, support for multiple programming languages offers great flexibility for developers with different preferences. Finally, QuantConnect benefits from an active and dynamic community that shares resources and contributes to the development of the platform, enriching the user experience.

However, there are a few points to consider before diving into using QuantConnect. Developing and testing algorithmic strategies requires programming knowledge, which can be an obstacle for some users. As with any trading platform, live trading always involves the risk of losing money. So it's crucial to manage expectations and understand that, while AI is a powerful tool, success in algorithmic trading requires a combination of strategy development, risk management and in-depth market knowledge.

In conclusion, QuantConnect is a valuable platform for those interested in algorithmic trading. Its open-source nature, cloud-based infrastructure and large community make it a good place to start. However, it's important to remember that algorithmic trading carries inherent risks and requires continuous learning and effort. For more information, please visit their website:

https://www.QuantConnect.com

Sentient Trader

- Sentient Trader is a software program designed for technical analysis of financial markets, specifically geared towards futures and forex trading [sentienttrader.com].

- It focuses on applying the Hurst Cycles analysis method, developed by J.M. Hurst, to identify potential trading opportunities.

How Does Sentient Trader Use AI (or Does it?)

There's some debate about whether Sentient Trader truly utilizes AI in the strictest sense. Here's what we know:

- Hurst Cycles Analysis: The Hurst Cycles method is a technical analysis approach based on cycles and ratios in market data. While it can involve calculations, it wouldn't be considered modern AI, which typically involves machine learning algorithms.

- Pattern Recognition: Sentient Trader might utilize some pattern recognition techniques to identify recurring patterns within Hurst Cycles analysis. However, the extent of this automation and its reliance on self-learning algorithms isn't entirely clear from available information.

Possible AI Applications (Speculative):

- Data Analysis Optimization: It's possible that Sentient Trader uses some basic AI in the background to optimize its analysis of Hurst Cycles data. This could involve filtering or weighting data points based on historical performance.

- Evolving Strategies: In theory, the software might have some level of adaptability based on past performance data. However, there's limited information on this aspect.

Here are some additional things to consider:

- Focus on User Interpretation: Sentient Trader seems to prioritize user interpretation of the analysis it provides. It might highlight potential trade opportunities, but the final decision rests with the user.

- Alternative AI Trading Platforms: If you're interested in exploring platforms that leverage more advanced AI for algorithmic trading, you might want to consider other options alongside Sentient Trader.

Robinhood AI Trading (Automation)

Robinhood's approach to AI trading seems to be rooted in the belief that the future of companies, including their own, lies in the integration and implementation of AI technologies. Robinhood's CEO, Vlad Tenev, has expressed that transitioning into an AI company is essential for staying ahead in the competitive landscape, indicating that AI will play a significant role in their long-term business model.
This might include the development of new products and features aimed at improving customer satisfaction and operational efficiency.

The use of AI in trading, particularly through Robinhood, extends to the use of crypto trading bots, which are designed to automate the trading process. These bots should be able to execute trades 24/7 based on predetermined criteria, without the need for manual intervention. They would offer features like automated trading strategies, risk management tools, real-time analytics, and robust security protocols to safeguard assets. These functionalities highlight the potential of AI to enhance trading efficiency and decision-making.

However, it's important to be aware of the risks and limitations associated with using automated trading systems. Technical failures, market volatility, and the need for continuous oversight are some of the key considerations. Despite the automation capabilities, traders are advised to remain informed about market conditions and adjust their strategies accordingly to navigate the unpredictable nature of cryptocurrency markets effectively.

Robinhood's foray into AI and the use of trading bots underscores the evolving landscape of financial trading, where technology and automation are becoming increasingly central. Yet, the emphasis on due diligence, strategy adjustment, and understanding the inherent risks of trading bots is a reminder of the complexity and challenges of navigating the crypto trading space.

Please note also that it's accurate to say that Robinhood does not currently offer built-in AI trading functionalities such as crypto trading bots directly within its platform.

Robinhood is primarily known for its commission-free stock and ETF trading services, aiming to democratize finance for all by providing a user-friendly interface that simplifies the investment process for retail investors. While the platform has been a pioneer in making trading accessible to a wider audience, its focus has been more on user experience and accessibility rather than offering advanced trading tools like AI-driven bots or automated trading strategies within its app.

Trading with AI

Robinhood's approach to trading emphasizes ease of use, aiming to attract and retain users who may be new to investing or prefer a straightforward platform for their trading needs. The emphasis is on manual trading, with features designed to support individual decision-making rather than automating trades based on algorithms or AI.

For users interested in more advanced trading tools, including those powered by AI, there are third-party services and platforms that offer such functionalities, which can sometimes be used in conjunction with Robinhood through APIs, albeit with caution due to potential policy restrictions or terms of service considerations.

Here are some third-party services and platforms that offer AI functionalities that you can potentially use in conjunction with your Robinhood account:

AI-powered Research and Analysis:

- **Equities.com**: This platform utilizes AI to analyze vast amounts of financial data and generate insights on publicly traded companies. It can provide AI-driven stock ratings, news **sentiment analysis**, and potential future price movements. You can use this information for research before making investment decisions on Robinhood.

- **MarketWatch**: While not purely AI-driven, MarketWatch offers a "Stocks Screener" tool that incorporates some AI filtering based on various criteria you set. This can help you narrow down potential stock picks for further research before trading on Robinhood.

- **TipRanks**: This platform aggregates stock ratings from analysts and combines them with AI-powered analysis of financial data, **news sentiment**, and social media buzz. This can offer a comprehensive overview of a stock before you invest through Robinhood.

- **TrendSpider**: This platform offers AI-powered technical analysis tools and identifies potential trading opportunities based on algorithmic analysis. You can use these insights to generate trading ideas, but remember to conduct your own research and analysis before executing trades on Robinhood.

Disclaimer: These are just a few examples, and it's important to conduct your own research on any platform before using it.

Sentiment Analysis Platforms

1. RavenPack

RavenPack is a leading provider of big data analytics for financial services. The platform analyzes structured and unstructured data, including news and social media, to generate real-time sentiment analysis. This analysis helps traders and portfolio managers make more informed decisions by providing insights into market sentiment that could affect asset prices.

2. Sentiment Trader

Sentiment Trader offers tools to visualize sentiment derived from social media, news, and fundamental data. Their AI analyzes vast amounts of data to offer traders insights into how sentiment is likely to influence different assets and markets. This is particularly useful for traders who need to quickly assess the impact of sentiment on market conditions.

3. Accern

Accern is a code-free AI platform that enhances workflow automation for financial services by monitoring news, blogs and social media in real time. Accern's sentiment analysis models can identify and categorize opinions in text data, helping traders understand market sentiment and potential impacts on their trading strategies.

4. Social Market Analytics (SMA)

SMA provides high-frequency sentiment data derived from social media. It quantifies the sentiment of tweets about financial markets, generating actionable signals that can inform trading decisions. SMA data streams are often integrated into quantitative models to improve the predictive power of market movements.

5. PsychSignal

PsychSignal offers trader sentiment analysis, translating social media data and other text into actionable sentiment scores. By analyzing chatter from sources such as Twitter and stock-specific forums, PsychSignal helps traders understand public sentiment towards particular stocks or the market in general.

6. Bloomberg Terminal

Although primarily known for its comprehensive financial data, Bloomberg Terminal also offers powerful sentiment analysis tools that analyze news and social media. These tools can help traders gain a more complete view of market conditions by understanding how sentiment is evolving and its potential effects on the market.

ZuluTrade (Social & Copy Trading)

ZuluTrade presents itself as a social trading and copy trading platform for forex and other markets. While they highlight the use of AI-powered trading strategies by some of their signal providers (the traders you can copy), it's important to understand the nuances.

ZuluTrade's use of AI is not a feature built into the entire platform. It is offered by individual traders (signal providers) who may use AI in their trading strategies. However, ZuluTrade does not necessarily disclose which signal providers use AI or the specific type of AI algorithms employed.

ZuluTrade allows you to connect and copy other traders' trades. These signal providers can employ a variety of trading strategies, including some that might use AI for analysis or signal generation. By choosing which signal providers to copy, you are ultimately responsible for the performance of your copied trades.

Important considerations with ZuluTrade and AI

When copying a signal provider, you're essentially entrusting them with control of your trades. It's crucial to choose reputable providers with a proven track record. Beware of signal providers making unrealistic promises of guaranteed profits. Past performance does not necessarily predict future results.

Even with AI-powered strategies, it's essential to thoroughly research signal providers before copying their trades. Understand their trading style, risk tolerance and historical performance.

ZuluTrade can be an interesting platform for exploring social trading and copy trading, but the use of AI depends on the individual signal providers, not the platform itself. Before copying trades, prioritize thorough research on signal providers and understand the inherent risks involved.

Integrating AI with Technical Analysis

In today's fast-paced and volatile market environment, non-professional traders are constantly seeking ways to improve their trading strategies and stay ahead of the curve. One of the most innovative and effective ways to do so is by integrating artificial intelligence (AI) with technical analysis.

Technical analysis has long been a popular tool used by traders to analyze past price movements and predict future price trends. By studying charts, patterns, and indicators, traders can make informed decisions about when to buy or sell a particular asset. However, technical analysis can be time-consuming and complex, requiring traders to have a deep understanding of market dynamics and trends.

By incorporating AI into technical analysis, non-professional traders can take their trading strategies to the next level. AI algorithms are capable of processing vast amounts of data at lightning speed, identifying patterns and trends that may be missed by human traders. This can help traders make more accurate and timely decisions, increasing their chances of success in the market.

There are several ways in which AI can be integrated with technical analysis. For example, AI-powered trading platforms can analyze historical data to identify patterns and trends, and make real-time trading recommendations based on this analysis. AI can also be used to develop predictive models that can forecast future price movements with a high degree of accuracy.

By leveraging the power of AI in their trading strategies, non-professional traders can gain a competitive edge in the market and increase their chances of success. With the right tools and knowledge, traders can harness the power of AI to make more informed and profitable trading decisions.

A good example of this type of use is : **CentralCharts**.

Understanding Lutessia: The AI of CentralCharts

Introduction to Lutessia

Lutessia is an advanced AI tool integrated into the CentralCharts platform, designed to enhance the technical analysis capabilities for traders. It uses machine learning algorithms to analyze historical data, predict future market movements, and provide actionable trading insights. This AI system is tailored to assist both novice and experienced traders by automating complex analysis processes and delivering personalized recommendations.

How Lutessia Works

1. Data Analysis and Pattern Recognition: Lutessia processes vast amounts of historical market data to identify patterns and trends. This includes price movements, volume changes, and other relevant market indicators. The AI uses sophisticated algorithms to detect recurring patterns that might indicate potential future movements.

2. Machine Learning Models: The core of Lutessia's functionality lies in its machine learning models, which are trained on years of market data. These models are continually refined as new data becomes available, ensuring that the AI's predictions and analyses remain relevant and accurate.

3. Integration with Technical Indicators: Lutessia incorporates standard technical indicators into its analysis, such as Moving Averages, RSI, and MACD. By combining these traditional tools with AI-driven insights, the platform provides a robust analysis that enhances the predictive accuracy.

4. Real-Time Analysis and Recommendations: The AI analyzes market conditions in real-time and provides recommendations based on current market trends. These recommendations include potential entry and exit points, risk assessments, and suggested stop-loss and take-profit levels.

Benefits of Using Lutessia for Technical Analysis

Enhanced Accuracy: Lutessia's use of AI and machine learning offers a higher level of accuracy in predictions and market analysis compared to traditional methods alone. This can significantly benefit traders by reducing the likelihood of false signals and improving the success rate of trades.

Time Efficiency: By automating the analysis process, Lutessia saves traders significant amounts of time. This allows users to focus more on strategy optimization and less on the labor-intensive process of data analysis.

Personalized Trading Insights: Lutessia can tailor its analysis and recommendations based on the individual trading style and risk tolerance of each user. This personalization makes it a versatile tool suitable for a diverse range of trading strategies.

Risk Management: The AI provides detailed risk assessment tools that help traders manage and mitigate potential losses. By analyzing historical data and current market conditions, Lutessia can suggest optimal risk management strategies tailored to specific trades.

Examples of Results Using Lutessia

Example 1: Day Trading in Stock Markets Consider a day trader focusing on the technology sector. Lutessia identifies a breakout pattern in the stock of a leading tech company following a positive earnings report. The AI suggests buying the stock at $150 with a stop loss at $147 and a target sell price at $160. The trader follows the AI's recommendation, and the stock reaches the target within the trading day, resulting in a successful short-term gain.

Scenario Overview

Cryptocurrency markets are known for their volatility and rapid price changes. In this example, let's consider a trader using Lutessia to trade Bitcoin (BTC), aiming to capitalize on short-term price movements.

Initial Analysis

The trader starts by analyzing Bitcoin's recent market activity through Lutessia. The AI tool assesses historical data, recent price trends, trading volume, and applies technical indicators to establish a comprehensive market outlook.

Lutessia's Predictive Insights

Using its machine learning algorithms, Lutessia identifies a potential bullish pattern developing based on the convergence of several indicators:

- Moving Average Crossover: The 50-day moving average (MA) crosses above the 200-day MA, a traditional signal of potential bullish momentum.

- RSI (Relative Strength Index): RSI moves above 60, suggesting increasing buying momentum without entering overbought territory.

- MACD (Moving Average Convergence Divergence): The MACD line crosses above the signal line, indicating a buying opportunity.

Real-Time Analysis

As the market opens, Bitcoin shows a slight dip in price, which Lutessia identifies as a typical "pullback" in a bullish market. The AI recommends using this pullback as a buying opportunity.

Trading Strategy Recommendation

Based on the current market analysis, Lutessia suggests the following trade setup:

- Entry Point: Buy BTC at the current market price of $35,000.

- Stop-Loss Order: Set a stop-loss at $34,000 to limit potential losses if the market unexpectedly reverses.

- Take-Profit Order: Set an initial take-profit at $37,000 to secure gains.

Lutessia also provides a risk assessment indicating a moderate risk due to market volatility, with additional recommendations for adjusting the trade:

- If the price reaches $36,500 before hitting the take-profit, adjust the stop-loss to the entry point to break even.

- Consider selling 50% of the position at $36,500 to lock in partial profits and let the remainder run to $37,000.

Trade Execution and Outcome

The trader follows Lutessia's recommendations:

- Buy: The trader enters the market at $35,000 during the pullback.

- Adjustment: As the market approaches $36,500, the trader follows the AI's advice to adjust the stop-loss and sell half the position.

- Final Outcome: Bitcoin reaches the take-profit level at $37,000 later that day. The adjusted strategy secures profits while protecting the position from a potential reversal.

In this scenario, Lutessia's AI-driven analysis allows the trader to make informed, strategic decisions in the volatile cryptocurrency market. By leveraging real-time data, predictive analytics, and risk management recommendations, the trader efficiently capitalizes on market movements with enhanced confidence. This example underscores Lutessia's utility in providing actionable insights and tailored trading strategies that adapt to dynamic market conditions, particularly in the high-stakes environment of cryptocurrency trading.

Conclusion

Lutessia provides a powerful tool for traders looking to leverage AI capabilities in their trading strategy. With its advanced data analysis, real-time recommendations, and personalized insights, it offers a substantial advantage in navigating the complexities of various financial markets. Whether for day trading, swing trading, or long-term investment strategies, Lutessia's AI-driven approach enhances decision-making and can lead to more profitable trading outcomes.

Please note that Lutessia is in french.
Lutessia, while originally developed in French and primarily serving French-speaking traders, has equivalents available in several other major languages to cater to a global

audience. This expansion ensures that traders around the world can utilize the powerful AI-driven tools offered by CentralCharts in their native languages, enhancing accessibility and usability. Below are the names of Lutessia's equivalents in english, spanish, german and italian languages: Londinia, Madritia, Berolinia, Romia.

Libertify and Boursorama (Reco marketed)

Libertify[1] is an artificial intelligence platform used by Boursorama to better inform its users by analyzing market trends and relevant news. It offers recommendations based on news that can positively or negatively influence stock values, and also incorporates succinct technical analysis to identify resistance levels to watch out for.

Libertify doesn't just identify stocks that are likely to go up; it also flags assets at risk of depreciation. By combining current market trends with technical analysis, Libertify helps investors make 'informed' buy and sell decisions.

It's actually a partnership between Boursorama and Libertify, a company founded by a former founder of Pixmania, Deezer... , i.e. a company recognized[2] for its risk management and investment advisory tools, particularly in the cryptocurrency space. The company was honored in the Fast Track Hong Kong FinTech in Paris competition, highlighting its potential to transform the fintech landscape. Libertify offers tools that help identify and manage risk according to users' risk profiles, and integrates behavioral science techniques to continuously adjust these profiles.

Compared to the videos on the Boursorama website, where we see an Artificial Intelligence 'Libertify' embodied by a virtual presenter typical of today's AI personifications, it seems to be mostly 'communication' to make stock market trend suggestions relatively simple, and accessible to individual traders.

For Boursorama users considering Libertify, it's important to bear in mind that, while this technology can offer interesting insights, it should be used as a complement to other sources of information and in-depth personal analysis. Libertify's integration with Boursorama aims to provide investment advice and technical analysis, but it is essential to check the robustness of the data and remain critical of the recommendations provided.

In conclusion, while Libertify and Boursorama can offer useful tools for investors, it's crucial to take this advice with caution and not rely solely on these pretty appearances when making important financial decisions.

---

[1] https://www.boursorama.com/videos/tv/videos-intelligence-artificielle
[2] https://www.business2community.com/trading/libertify-review

Using AI for Risk Management

In the world of trading, risk management is crucial for success. With the advancement of technology, artificial intelligence (AI) has become a powerful tool for everyday traders to enhance their risk management strategies. By utilizing AI in your trading approach, you can effectively mitigate risks and make more informed decisions.

One of the key ways AI can be used for risk management is through predictive analytics. AI algorithms can analyze vast amounts of data to identify patterns and trends that may indicate potential risks in the market. By utilizing this predictive power, traders can proactively adjust their strategies to minimize potential losses.

Another way AI can help with risk management is through automated trading systems. These systems use AI algorithms to execute trades based on predefined rules and parameters. By automating the trading process, traders can reduce the emotional aspect of decision-making, which can often lead to impulsive and risky choices.

Furthermore, AI can also be used to create risk models that assess the probability of different outcomes in the market. By incorporating these models into your trading strategy, you can better understand the potential risks associated with each trade and make more informed decisions.

Overall, by incorporating AI into your risk management strategy, you can enhance your trading approach and improve your chances of success in the market. Whether you are a novice trader or have some experience in the field, utilizing AI for risk management can help you navigate the complexities of the market and make more profitable trades.

Chapter 4:
Case Studies of Successful AI Traders

Hedge Funds Using AI for Trading

In the fast-paced world of trading, hedge funds are constantly seeking new ways to gain an edge over the competition. One of the most powerful tools they have at their disposal is artificial intelligence (AI). By harnessing the power of AI, hedge funds can analyze vast amounts of data in real-time, identify patterns, and make more informed trading decisions.

AI has revolutionized the way hedge funds operate, allowing them to automate trading strategies and execute trades with lightning speed. This gives them a significant advantage in the market, as they can react to market conditions quicker than human traders ever could.

One of the key ways hedge funds are using AI for trading is through algorithmic trading. These algorithms can analyze market data and execute trades without any human intervention, allowing hedge funds to take advantage of opportunities in the market 24/7.

Another way AI is being used by hedge funds is through sentiment analysis. By analyzing social media posts, news articles, and other sources of information, AI can gauge market sentiment and make predictions about how certain assets will perform in the future.

For non-professional traders looking to incorporate AI into their trading strategy, studying how hedge funds use AI can provide valuable insights. While individual traders may not have access to the same level of resources as hedge funds, there are still ways to utilize AI to improve trading performance.

By leveraging AI tools and platforms, non-professional traders can gain access to sophisticated algorithms and data analysis techniques that can help them make more informed trading decisions. With the right approach, AI can be a powerful tool for everyday traders looking to stay ahead of the curve in an increasingly competitive market.

Retail Traders Incorporating AI in Their Strategies

In recent years, there has been a significant shift in the way retail traders approach the financial markets. With the advent of artificial intelligence (AI) technology, many non-professional traders are now incorporating AI into their trading strategies to gain a competitive edge.

Retail traders are increasingly turning to AI tools and algorithms to help them make more informed trading decisions. These AI systems can analyze vast amounts of data at speeds far beyond human capabilities, allowing traders to identify patterns and trends that may not be apparent to the naked eye.

One of the key ways that retail traders are incorporating AI into their strategies is through the use of automated trading systems. These systems use AI algorithms to execute trades on behalf of the trader, based on pre-defined rules and parameters. This can help traders take emotion out of the trading equation and stick to their strategy even in volatile market conditions.

Another way that retail traders are leveraging AI is through the use of predictive analytics. By analyzing historical data and market trends, AI algorithms can help traders forecast future price movements with a higher degree of accuracy. This can help traders make more informed decisions about when to enter or exit a trade, potentially increasing their profits.

Overall, the use of AI in trading has the potential to level the playing field for non-professional traders, allowing them to compete more effectively with institutional investors and professional traders. By incorporating AI into their trading strategies, retail traders can harness the power of technology to improve their trading performance and achieve their financial goals.

Real-Life Examples of AI Improving Trading Performance

In the world of trading, the use of artificial intelligence (AI) has become increasingly prevalent. Non-professional traders are now able to harness the power of AI to improve their trading performance and make more informed decisions. In this subchapter, we will explore real-life examples of how AI has been successfully utilized to enhance trading strategies.

One prominent example of AI improving trading performance is the use of machine learning algorithms to analyze vast amounts of data and identify patterns that human traders may overlook. These algorithms can process information at speeds far beyond human capabilities, allowing traders to make split-second decisions based on real-time market data.

Another example is the use of natural language processing (NLP) technology to analyze news articles, social media posts, and other sources of information to gauge market sentiment. By understanding the prevailing sentiment in the market, traders can adjust their strategies accordingly and capitalize on market trends.

Furthermore, AI-powered trading platforms can automate the execution of trades based on predefined criteria, eliminating human error and emotions from the trading process. These platforms can also continuously monitor market conditions and adjust trading strategies in real-time to optimize performance.

Overall, the integration of AI into trading strategies has the potential to revolutionize the way non-professional traders approach the market. By leveraging the power of AI to analyze data, identify patterns, and make informed decisions, traders can improve their performance and achieve greater success in the increasingly competitive world of trading.

One famous person who has leveraged AI to improve trading performance is Ray Dalio, the founder of Bridgewater Associates, one of the world's largest hedge funds. Dalio is known for his use of AI and machine learning algorithms to analyze market data and make investment decisions.
Ray Dalio and his team at Bridgewater Associates developed a proprietary AI system called "Pure Alpha," which utilizes machine learning algorithms to analyze market trends, economic data, and other factors that may impact investment opportunities.

The AI system is able to process vast amounts of data in real-time and identify patterns and correlations that human traders may not be able to see.
By incorporating AI into their trading strategy, Bridgewater Associates has been able to achieve consistent and profitable returns for their investors.
The AI system helps the fund identify trading opportunities, manage risk, and optimize portfolio allocations, leading to improved overall performance.

One of the most impressive results of Ray Dalio's use of AI in trading is the performance of Bridgewater's flagship fund, the Pure Alpha II fund. Over the years, the fund has consistently outperformed market benchmarks and delivered strong returns to investors. For example, in 2020, the Pure Alpha II fund reportedly generated a return of over 14%, outperforming many other hedge funds and investment vehicles during a challenging market environment.

Ray Dalio's success in using AI for trading demonstrates the power of leveraging technology to enhance decision-making and drive better performance in the financial markets. By embracing AI and machine learning, traders and investors can gain valuable insights, identify profitable opportunities, and achieve superior results in their trading activities.

While Ray Dalio's success in using AI for trading at Bridgewater Associates is impressive, it is important to note that the strategies and technologies employed by large hedge funds like Bridgewater may not be directly applicable to personal trading for several reasons:

1. **Complexity**: The AI systems developed and used by large hedge funds like Bridgewater are often highly sophisticated and proprietary, requiring significant resources, expertise, and infrastructure to develop and maintain. These systems may not be easily accessible or practical for individual traders to replicate.
2. **Regulatory Considerations** : Institutional investors and hedge funds are subject to different regulatory requirements and oversight compared to individual traders. The use of AI in trading may be subject to compliance and reporting obligations that may not apply to personal trading activities.
3. **Risk Management** : Institutional investors like Bridgewater Associates have dedicated risk management teams and processes in place to oversee and control the risks associated with their trading activities. Personal traders may not have the same level of risk management infrastructure in place, making it important to consider the potential risks and challenges of using AI in personal trading.
4. **Scale** : Institutional investors like Bridgewater often operate on a much larger scale than individual traders, allowing them to access and analyze vast amounts of data and execute trades at high speeds. Personal traders may not have access to the same resources and market liquidity, which can impact the effectiveness of AI-driven trading strategies.

While individual traders can certainly benefit from incorporating AI tools and technologies into their trading activities, it is essential to consider the unique challenges and limitations that may apply to personal trading. It is recommended for personal traders to conduct thorough research, seek professional advice, and carefully assess the suitability and feasibility of using AI in their trading strategies.

Anyway, here are some real-life examples of how AI has been used to improve trading performance:

1. **Quantitative Hedge Funds** : Hedge funds such as Renaissance Technologies and Two Sigma have been using AI and machine learning algorithms for years to analyze vast amounts of financial data and identify profitable trading opportunities. These algorithms can quickly process complex data sets and make trades at high speeds, giving these funds a competitive advantage in the market.
2. **High-Frequency Trading** : High-frequency trading firms use AI-powered algorithms to execute trades in milliseconds based on real-time market data and signals. These algorithms can detect patterns and trends in the market that are difficult for human traders to spot, allowing firms to make fast and profitable trades.
3. **Robo-Advisors** : Robo-advisors, such as Wealthfront and Betterment, use AI algorithms to automate investment and trading decisions for individual investors. These platforms analyze an investor's financial goals, risk tolerance, and market conditions to create a customized investment portfolio and rebalance it as needed to optimize returns.
4. **Pattern Recognition** : AI algorithms can analyze historical market data to identify patterns and trends that human traders may overlook. By recognizing these patterns, traders can make more informed decisions about when to buy or sell assets, leading to improved trading performance.

5. **Sentiment Analysis** : AI tools can analyze news articles, social media posts, and other sources of market sentiment to gauge investor sentiment and predict market movements. By incorporating sentiment analysis into their trading strategies, investors can make better-informed decisions and react more quickly to changing market conditions.

These examples demonstrate the diverse ways in which AI is being used to enhance trading performance and improve decision-making in the financial markets. By leveraging the power of AI and machine learning, traders and investors can gain a competitive edge and achieve better outcomes in their trading activities.

So, what can be done at your individual level ?

Here are some accessible tools and websites that individual traders can use to enhance trading performance and improve decision-making in the financial markets:

1. Algorithmic Trading :

- **MetaTrader**: MetaTrader is a popular trading platform that offers algorithmic trading capabilities through its MetaTrader 4 and MetaTrader 5 platforms. Traders can use MetaTrader to develop, backtest, and deploy algorithmic trading strategies.

2. Predictive Analytics :

- **TradingView**: TradingView is a web-based platform that offers technical analysis tools and charting capabilities for traders. It also provides access to a community of traders who share trading ideas and strategies based on predictive analytics.

3. Sentiment Analysis :

- **Investing.com**: Investing.com offers a sentiment analysis tool that aggregates news articles, social media posts, and market data to provide insights into market sentiment. Traders can use this tool to gauge investor sentiment and make decisions based on market sentiment indicators, even if it is not yet true AI powered sentiment Analysis.

4. Portfolio Optimization :

- **Portfolio Visualizer**: Portfolio Visualizer is a free online tool that allows traders to analyze and optimize their investment portfolios. Traders can input their assets, risk tolerance, and investment goals to create diversified portfolios and analyze historical performance.

5. Risk Management :

- **MyFxBook**: MyFxBook is a risk management tool specifically designed for forex traders. It provides features such as trade analysis, risk calculators, and performance tracking to help traders manage their risk exposure and protect their investments.

These tools and websites offer accessible resources and capabilities for individual traders to enhance their trading performance, make more informed decisions, and manage risks in the financial markets. It is important for traders to research and understand how to use these tools effectively and to consider their own trading goals and strategies when incorporating them into their trading activities.

Some little focus

MetaTrader

MetaTrader, particularly MetaTrader 4 (MT4) and MetaTrader 5 (MT5), are popular forex and CFD trading platforms widely used by brokers and retail traders. While not inherently AI-powered themselves, MetaTrader offers functionalities that can be leveraged for AI-assisted trading:

MetaTrader's AI Capabilities

- Expert Advisors (EAs): These are automated trading scripts you can code or purchase from third-party developers. Some EAs might utilize machine learning or other AI techniques for algorithmic trading.

- MQL4/MQL5 Programming Languages: These languages allow you to develop custom trading strategies, potentially incorporating AI elements like sentiment analysis or price pattern recognition. However, coding knowledge is required.

- Limited Platform-Level AI (MT5): MetaTrader 5 offers a beta feature called "AI Code Assistant" for some users. This assistant provides suggestions to help with coding custom indicators and EAs, but it's not a full-fledged AI trading solution.

So what could be your benefits of Potentially Using AI with MetaTrader:

- Automated Trading: EAs can automate your trading strategy, potentially reducing the need for constant manual intervention.

- Backtesting and Optimization: AI-powered EAs can be backtested on historical data to optimize their performance before deploying them with real capital.

- Data Analysis and Pattern Recognition: AI can analyze vast amounts of market data to identify trading opportunities that might be difficult for humans to spot.

Important Considerations with AI and MetaTrader:

- Coding Knowledge Required: Developing or using AI-powered EAs often requires programming knowledge in MQL4/MQL5.

- Performance Not Guaranteed: AI-powered EAs are not fail-proof. Markets are unpredictable, and even with AI, losses can still occur.

- Regulation and Risk Management: Ensure your chosen broker allows algorithmic trading and has proper risk management measures in place.

MetaTrader itself isn't inherently AI-powered, but its functionalities like EAs and programming languages allow for the use of custom AI-assisted trading strategies. However, this approach requires coding knowledge and carries inherent risks. Consider your skillset, risk tolerance, and explore alternative platforms or managed accounts before diving into AI for trading with MetaTrader.

TradingViews

TradingView is a well-regarded web-based charting platform for stock, forex, and other asset classes. It offers a variety of features for technical analysis, charting, and social networking for traders. While TradingView doesn't offer fully automated AI trading, it does incorporate some AI functionalities that can be helpful for traders:

TradingView's AI Uses:

- AI-powered Indicators: TradingView offers a library of technical indicators, some of which are labeled as "AI" or "Machine Learning" indicators. These indicators might use algorithms to analyze historical price data, identify patterns, and generate trading signals.

- Strategy Tester with AI Optimization (Limited): The platform's strategy tester allows you to backtest your trading strategies on historical data. Some paid plans offer limited features for AI-powered optimization of these strategies, but it's not a fully automated process.

- Pattern Recognition and Alerts: Some AI-powered indicators might use pattern recognition techniques to identify potential trading opportunities and generate alerts based on those patterns.

Important Considerations with TradingView's AI:

- Not Fully Automated Trading: TradingView doesn't offer features for fully automated trading based on AI signals. You'll need to make your own trading decisions based on the generated signals.

- Limited Transparency: TradingView doesn't always disclose the specific details behind the algorithms used in its AI-powered indicators.

- Backtesting Limitations: AI-powered strategy optimization is a limited feature on higher-tier paid plans.

TradingView's AI features can be a helpful addition to your technical analysis toolbox. They can spark new ideas, aid in pattern recognition, and help refine your strategies. However, remember these functionalities are for informational purposes and shouldn't be the sole basis for your trading decisions.

You should also explore Free vs Paid Plans: The extent of AI features depends on your TradingView subscription plan.

Investing.com

Investing.com offers a feature called "Community Sentiments Outlook," but it's important to clarify that this isn't exactly sentiment analysis AI in the traditional sense. Here's a breakdown:

Investing.com's Community Sentiment:

- User Votes: This feature relies on votes cast by individual users on the platform regarding their sentiment (bullish or bearish) on various financial instruments like stocks, currencies, or commodities.

- Gauge of Market Opinion: It provides a general indication of the overall bullish or bearish sentiment among the Investing.com user community for a particular asset.

Not AI-powered Sentiment Analysis:

- No Algorithmic Analysis: The platform doesn't use any AI algorithms to analyze news articles, social media, or other data sources to gauge sentiment.

- Limited Scope: It only reflects the sentiment of users who actively participate on the platform, and may not represent the broader market sentiment.

However, Investing.com does offer other features that might be relevant:

- News & Analysis Section: This section provides access to financial news articles, which can help you understand the factors influencing market sentiment.
- Technical Analysis Tools: The platform offers various technical analysis tools that can be used to identify potential trading opportunities, although these don't directly incorporate sentiment analysis.
- **Investing proposes also some AI driven recommendations built on long history of data.**

Here's a comparison of Investing.com's sentiment feature with true sentiment analysis AI:

Feature	Investing.com's Community Sentiment	AI-powered Sentiment Analysis
Functionality	User votes on bullish or bearish sentiment	Analyzes news articles, social media, and other data sources
Data Source	Investing.com user base	Publicly available financial data, social media feeds, news articles
Insights	General user sentiment on the platform	In-depth analysis of market sentiment and potential underlying factors

While Investing.com's Community Sentiment offers a glimpse into user sentiment, it's not a substitute for true AI-powered sentiment analysis. Consider these points:

- Limited Scope: Relying solely on user votes might not provide an accurate picture of the broader market sentiment.

- Combine with Other Research: Use this feature alongside other research methods like news analysis and technical analysis for a more comprehensive understanding of the market.

- True AI Sentiment Analysis Tools: Explore platforms that offer AI-powered sentiment analysis tools that analyze a wider range of data sources for a more in-depth view.

Here are some platforms that offer AI-powered sentiment analysis tools for trading:

Platforms with Built-in AI Sentiment Analysis:

- **Syntopia**: This platform focuses on social media sentiment analysis using AI to gauge market sentiment from social media conversations. It can help identify potential trends and shifts in investor confidence.

- **Kensho**: This platform utilizes AI to analyze vast amounts of financial data, including news articles, social media, and regulatory filings. It provides sentiment analysis alongside other insights to help identify potential trading opportunities.

- **Lexalytics**: This platform offers a suite of AI-powered text analytics tools, including sentiment analysis. It can be integrated with trading platforms to provide real-time sentiment analysis of news feeds and social media related to specific assets.

Trading Platforms with AI Sentiment Analysis Integrations:

- **TradeStation**: This trading platform offers its own sentiment analysis tools and integrates with some third-party AI-powered sentiment analysis platforms for a more comprehensive view.

- **Interactive Brokers**: This broker provides access to various research tools, including some that incorporate AI-powered sentiment analysis from external sources.

Considerations When Choosing a Platform:

- Data Sources Analyzed: Understand what data sources (news, social media, etc.) the AI tool analyzes for sentiment.

- Customization Options: See if the platform allows you to customize the sentiment analysis to focus on specific assets or news sources.

- Integration with Trading Tools: If you use a particular trading platform, check if the AI sentiment analysis tool integrates with it for seamless workflow.

- Cost and Free Trials: These platforms often have different pricing structures. Look for free trials or demos to test their functionalities before committing.

By understanding the capabilities and limitations of these AI-powered sentiment analysis tools, you can potentially enhance your research and make more informed trading decisions.

Chapter 5:
Overcoming Challenges of Using AI in Trading

Data Privacy and Security leak, true story

One notable example of a data privacy and security breach that occurred in the trading industry is the case of the 2010 "Flash Crash." On May 6, 2010, the U.S. stock market experienced a sudden and severe drop in prices, followed by a rapid recovery, in what became known as the Flash Crash. It was later revealed that the Flash Crash was triggered by a single large sell order in the futures market, which was executed by an algorithmic trading program.

The algorithm used in this case belonged to a trader named Navinder Singh Sarao, who operated from his home in the UK. Sarao's algorithm was designed to place and cancel large sell orders in the E-mini S&P 500 futures market, creating the appearance of market activity without actually executing trades. This practice, known as "spoofing," is illegal under U.S. securities laws.

Sarao's actions contributed to the extreme volatility and rapid price movements that led to the Flash Crash. Following an investigation by U.S. authorities, Sarao was charged with multiple counts of fraud and market manipulation. In 2016, he pleaded guilty to spoofing and wire fraud charges and was sentenced to prison.

The Flash Crash incident highlighted the risks associated with algorithmic trading and the potential for data privacy and security breaches in the trading industry. It underscored the importance of implementing robust risk management controls, monitoring systems, and regulatory oversight to prevent market manipulation and ensure the integrity of financial markets. Traders and financial institutions must remain vigilant in safeguarding sensitive market data and ensuring compliance with regulatory requirements to protect against data privacy and security breaches in the trading industry.

Data Privacy and Security Concerns

In the world of trading with AI, one of the most pressing issues that non-professional traders need to be aware of is data privacy and security concerns. As artificial intelligence continues to play an increasingly important role in trading strategies, it is crucial for traders to understand the potential risks associated with using AI in their everyday trading activities.

One of the main concerns surrounding data privacy and security in the context of AI trading is the protection of sensitive personal and financial information. When utilizing AI algorithms to make trading decisions, traders must ensure that their data is being handled securely and responsibly. This includes encrypting data transmissions, implementing robust authentication measures, and regularly updating security protocols to guard against potential cyber threats.

Another key consideration for non-professional traders is the potential for data breaches and unauthorized access to trading algorithms. With the increasing sophistication of cyber attacks, traders must be vigilant in protecting their AI trading strategies from malicious actors who may seek to exploit vulnerabilities in their systems. This can involve regularly monitoring system logs, conducting security audits, and implementing multi-factor authentication to prevent unauthorized access.

Furthermore, traders must also consider the ethical implications of using AI in their trading activities. As AI algorithms become increasingly complex and autonomous, there is a risk that they may inadvertently make decisions that are biased or discriminatory. Traders must be mindful of the potential for algorithmic bias and take steps to mitigate these risks by regularly auditing their AI systems and ensuring that their trading strategies are fair and transparent.

In conclusion, data privacy and security concerns are paramount for non-professional traders looking to leverage AI in their trading strategies. By taking proactive measures to protect their data, guard against potential cyber threats, and mitigate algorithmic bias, traders can ensure that they are using AI responsibly and ethically in their everyday trading activities.

Handling Market Volatility with AI

In the world of trading, market volatility can be both a blessing and a curse. While it presents opportunities for significant gains, it also comes with a high level of risk. For non-professional traders looking to navigate this uncertainty, AI can be a valuable tool.

One of the key benefits of AI in trading is its ability to handle market volatility with ease. Unlike human traders who may be swayed by emotions or make rash decisions in the face of fluctuating markets, AI systems can analyze vast amounts of data in real-time and make informed, data-driven decisions.

AI algorithms can quickly adapt to changing market conditions and adjust trading strategies accordingly. This allows non-professional traders to stay ahead of the curve and capitalize on opportunities that may arise during periods of volatility. By using AI, traders can take advantage of market fluctuations and potentially increase their profits while minimizing their risks.

Furthermore, AI can help traders identify patterns and trends in the market that may not be immediately apparent to the human eye. By leveraging machine learning algorithms, traders can gain insights into market behavior and make more informed decisions about when to buy or sell.

Overall, incorporating AI into your trading strategy can help you navigate market volatility more effectively and improve your overall trading performance. By utilizing the power of AI, non-professional traders can level the playing field and compete more effectively in today's fast-paced and unpredictable markets.

Balancing Human Decision-Making with AI Recommendations

In the world of trading, the use of artificial intelligence (AI) has become increasingly popular among non-professional traders looking to improve their trading strategies. However, one of the key challenges that traders face when integrating AI into their decision-making process is finding the right balance between human judgment and AI recommendations.

While AI can provide valuable insights and recommendations based on data analysis and algorithms, it is important for traders to remember that human intuition and experience also play a crucial role in making successful trades. This is why finding the right balance between human decision-making and AI recommendations is essential for maximizing trading success.

One way to achieve this balance is to use AI as a tool to complement your own analysis and decision-making process. By leveraging AI to identify patterns and trends in the market, traders can gain valuable insights that may not be immediately apparent to the human eye. However, it is important to remember that AI is not infallible and should be used as a guide rather than a definitive answer.

Another important aspect of balancing human decision-making with AI recommendations is to continuously monitor and evaluate the performance of your trading strategy. By keeping a close eye on how your trades are performing and adjusting your approach as needed, you can ensure that you are making informed decisions based on a combination of AI insights and human judgment.

Ultimately, finding the right balance between human decision-making and AI recommendations is a key factor in achieving success as a non-professional trader. By leveraging the strengths of both AI and human intuition, traders can make more informed decisions and improve their overall trading strategy.

Chapter 6 : Utilizing AI for Trading Specific Financial Products

This chapter explores the transformative potential of artificial intelligence in trading various financial products. By understanding the unique characteristics of each product, traders can leverage the right AI tools to enhance their trading strategies, minimize risks, and maximize returns.

1. Trading Futures with AI

What are Futures?

Futures are standardized contracts that obligate the buyer to purchase and the seller to sell a specified quantity of an asset at a predetermined price on a specified future date. These are traded across various asset classes, including commodities, currencies, and financial instruments.

Unlike options, which give the holder the right but not the obligation to buy or sell the asset, futures contracts impose strict obligations on both parties involved.

Futures are commonly used for hedging risk or speculating on the price movement of the underlying asset. For example, a farmer might use futures to lock in a price for his crop months before it is harvested. Conversely, a trader might speculate on the future price of oil or a currency, hoping to profit from price movements.

By using futures contracts, both hedgers and speculators can manage their exposure to price volatility of the underlying assets, providing a measure of financial predictability and security in their commercial activities or investment portfolios.

AI Strategies for Futures Trading

AI can significantly enhance futures trading through predictive analytics and automated trading systems. These tools can analyze market trends and execute trades based on optimized algorithms.

Trading with AI

Concerning **Trend Prediction and Pattern Recognition**, AI models, particularly those involving machine learning, can analyze vast amounts of historical and real-time data to identify underlying patterns and predict future market trends. This can be particularly useful in futures markets where price movements are influenced by various factors like economic indicators, geopolitical events, and market sentiment.
Example: An AI system might analyze decades of oil futures data, including responses to geopolitical events, supply changes, and demand fluctuations, to predict how prices might respond to similar future events. By training on historical data, the AI model can forecast price movements with a higher degree of accuracy, enabling traders to make informed decisions about entry and exit points.

Concerning **Automated Trading Systems**, they can execute trades based on criteria set by the trader, using algorithms that can adapt to changing market conditions without human intervention. These systems can process data at a speed and accuracy that is impossible for human traders, making them particularly useful in the highly volatile futures market.
Example: A trader uses an AI-driven trading system on the Chicago Mercantile Exchange to trade S&P 500 futures. The AI system is programmed to execute trades based on specific market indicators such as moving averages and volatility indexes. When the AI detects a pattern that historically precedes a price increase, it automatically buys futures, and conversely, it sells futures when predicting a price drop.

Concerning **Risk Management and Mitigation**, AI can significantly improve risk management in futures trading by predicting potential price drops and advising on risk exposure. Advanced AI models can simulate various market scenarios and predict outcomes based on historical volatility, market cycles, and external economic factors.
Example: An AI model might analyze the impact of interest rate changes on commodity futures. If the model predicts a high risk of price decline due to an impending rate hike, it can automatically adjust the trader's portfolio to reduce exposure to affected commodities, thereby mitigating potential losses.

Concerning **Sentiment analysis**, using AI can parse through vast amounts of news articles, social media posts, and financial reports to gauge market sentiment. This can be particularly useful for futures trading, where market sentiment can significantly influence price.
Example: Before an OPEC meeting, an AI system analyzes thousands of news articles and social media posts to gauge the market sentiment regarding potential oil supply cuts. If the sentiment is strongly indicative of a substantial cut, the AI might suggest buying oil futures before the meeting, anticipating a rise in oil prices.

Concerning **Backtesting Strategies**, AI can automate the backtesting of trading strategies over historical data, providing insights into their effectiveness and resilience under different market conditions. This allows traders to refine their strategies before applying them in live trading. Example: A trader develops a new trading strategy for gold futures and uses AI to backtest this strategy using historical data from the past 20 years. The AI assesses the strategy's performance across various market conditions, including recessions and booms, and provides feedback on its viability and potential risk factors.

Best AI Tools for Futures

QuantConnect As we saw, QuantConnect allows traders to backtest and live-trade their futures strategies using historical data.

Success Story: A group of algorithmic traders used QuantConnect to develop a diversified commodity futures strategy that significantly outperformed the benchmark over a two-year period. The strategy utilized trend-following signals combined with mean reversion setups to capture short-term anomalies in the market.

TradeStation is renowned for its advanced trading capabilities and real-time data processing, essential for the rapid movements in futures markets.

Success Story: A trader automated a scalping strategy on TradeStation, capitalizing on small price gaps in the S&P 500 futures, significantly enhancing trade execution and profit margins.

2. Trading Warrants & Turbos with AI

What are Warrants & Turbos?

Warrants and turbos are derivative instruments that allow traders to speculate on the price movements of an underlying asset with leverage. Turbos, in particular, **offer high leverage** with a built-in stop-loss feature.

AI Strategies for Warrants & Turbos

Leveraging AI for sentiment analysis and risk assessment can provide traders with a significant edge in these highly volatile instruments..

I am particularly enthusiastic about using warrant calls or puts as part of my trading strategy, especially when AI tools help in identifying clear trends in stock movements. Warrants can significantly amplify potential gains when a reliable trend is detected, making them an exciting option for traders.

When using AI to identify trends, it's important to choose warrants judiciously to maximize the benefits while managing risks effectively. I always recommend selecting warrants with expiration dates that are more than three months away. This longer time frame provides an additional cushion, allowing for recovery and adjustment if the initial trend prediction doesn't immediately pan out as expected.

Additionally, I focus on warrants with a delta between 25% and 80%. This range typically offers a good balance of risk and potential return, ensuring that the warrants are sufficiently responsive to the underlying asset's price movements but not so sensitive that minor price fluctuations could result in significant losses.

By adhering to these guidelines and utilizing AI to assist in trend analysis, traders can strategically position themselves to capitalize on market movements while affording themselves an extra margin for error, should the market behave unpredictably. This approach allows for leveraging the potential high returns of warrants with a more calculated risk, adapting over time as market conditions evolve.

Best AI Tools for Warrants & Turbos

Sentdex analyzes financial sentiment from various media sources to gauge market mood, which is particularly useful for trading warrants and turbos.
Success Story: An investment rm used Sentdex to detect a positive sentiment spike in tech stocks, timing their warrant purchases before significant price increases.

Riskalyze assesses investment risk aligned with a trader's risk tolerance, crucial for managing the inherent risks of turbos.
Success Story: Using Riskalyze, a retail investor identified an overexposure to volatility in their portfolio, allowing timely adjustments that mitigated potential significant losses during a market downturn.

3. Trading ETFs with AI

What are ETFs?

Exchange-Traded Funds (ETFs) are investment funds traded on stock exchanges, much like stocks. They hold assets such as stocks, commodities, or bonds and typically track an index.

AI Strategies for ETF Trading

AI-driven portfolio optimization and trend analysis tools can help traders manage ETF investments more effectively, adjusting holdings to maximize returns and reduce risks.

Best AI Tools for ETFs

Betterment uses AI to manage ETF investments, optimizing asset allocation based on individual goals and market conditions.
Success Story: A retiree's ETF portfolio managed by Betterment navigated the volatility of the COVID-19 market crash more effectively than traditional investment strategies, preserving capital and capturing recovery gains.

Wealthfront offers automated financial planning and investment management, ideal for dynamically managing ETF portfolios.

Success Story: A young professional used Wealthfront to build a diversified ETF portfolio that outperformed standard benchmarks through strategic international and sector-specific allocations.

Recommended Reading for ETF Enthusiasts

If you are curious about exploring the world of Exchange-Traded Funds (ETFs) and wish to deepen your understanding, I highly recommend reading the works of Edouard Petit.

His book offers comprehensive insights into the mechanisms, strategies, and benefits of investing in ETFs. Edouard Petit's clear explanations and expert advice make his book an invaluable resource for both novice investors and seasoned traders looking to enhance their ETF portfolios.

Dive into his writings to expand your knowledge and rene your investment strategies in the dynamic world of ETFs.

While Edouard Petit's books, "Tout savoir sur les ETF et les fonds indiciels" and "Epargnant 3.0," are excellent resources for understanding ETFs and modern investment strategies, it's important to note that they do not specifically address Artificial Intelligence (AI) in trading or investment management. Edouard Petit's work focuses primarily on the fundamentals of ETFs, their strategic use in personal finance, and how individual investors can leverage these tools to optimize their portfolios.

4. Trading Forex with AI

Cautionary Note on Forex Trading and AI Tools

While discussing the application of AI in various trading platforms, it's important to address the Forex market specifically. I want to emphasize that I am not a fan of Forex trading for several reasons, primarily due to the significant risks it poses to retail investors.

Forex trading involves substantial risk and complexity, particularly because it often encourages the use of high leverage. Such leverage can amplify gains but more frequently exacerbates losses, especially in volatile markets. The Forex market operates 24 hours a day and is influenced by a myriad of factors that can be difficult to track and predict, even with advanced tools.

Many platforms and tools advertise the potential for high returns in Forex trading using AI-driven strategies. However, traders should approach these claims with caution. It is important to note that a large portion of AI Forex platforms might not necessarily align with the users' best interests. Some of these platforms are not transparent about their operations and may have underlying motives centered around user transaction fees or worse, could be outright scams.

Statistically, the success rate for retail Forex traders is low. Various reports and studies suggest that more than 70% of Forex traders lose money, with a significant portion of these losses attributed to the misuse of leverage. These statistics highlight the exceptional challenges of achieving consistent profitability in Forex trading.

Recommendations for Traders

For those considering Forex, or any platform purporting to use AI to enhance Forex trading:

- Research Thoroughly: Always research any platform or tool extensively. Look for reviews, regulatory compliance, and transparency in operations.

- Be Wary of Promises: Be skeptical of claims promising guaranteed returns or minimal risks. Trading always involves risk, particularly in Forex.

- Educate Yourself: Understand the market dynamics and the tools you plan to use. The more informed you are, the better equipped you'll be to make safe trading decisions.

- Use Demo Accounts: Before committing real money, practice with demo accounts offered by reputable platforms to understand the risk and reality of Forex trading without financial exposure.

  While AI can offer significant advantages in data processing and decision-making in trading, its application in Forex requires careful consideration due to the inherent risks and the prevalence of misleading platforms. If you decide to venture into Forex trading, proceed with caution, prioritize learning, and always prioritize your financial safety.

What is Forex?

The Forex market is the largest and most liquid financial market globally, where currencies are traded 24 hours a day. It involves high levels of liquidity and rapid price movements.

AI Strategies for Forex Trading

Forex trading can benefit immensely from AI through predictive analytics and automated trading algorithms, which can analyze multiple currency pairs and execute trades based on complex market indicators.

Best AI Tools for Forex

MetaTrader 4 and 5 support automated trading with Expert Advisors (EAs), enabling traders to implement sophisticated trading strategies in the Forex market.
 Success Story: A Forex trader developed an EA for MetaTrader 4 that traded based on daily pivot points and Fibonacci retracement levels. This EA consistently outperformed manual trading efforts, leading to a 20% increase in annual profits.

OANDA provides powerful Forex trading tools with advanced charting and AI analytics, perfect for crafting precise trading strategies.
 Success Story: Utilizing OANDA's AI-driven platform, a trading firm developed a model that predicted short-term currency movements based on geopolitical events and economic indicators. The model's accurate predictions resulted in a 30% improvement in trading efficiency.

Conclusion

AI has the potential to revolutionize trading across different financial products by providing powerful tools for analysis, prediction, and risk management. Traders are encouraged to explore these AI applications to enhance their decision-making processes, adapt to market changes quickly, and achieve sustained success in their trading endeavors.

Chapter 7:
AI and Social Media in Analyzing Stock Market Trends

Introduction

Social media platforms such as TikTok and Instagram have transformed the landscape of stock trading by democratizing access to information and influencing investment decisions. These platforms, where millions of amateur traders share advice and trends, have become powerful tools for anticipating market movements. Artificial Intelligence (AI) can play a crucial role in analyzing these vast data streams to identify market trends and investment opportunities.

Social Media: A New Arena for Investments

Social media enables financial influencers to share their analyses and forecasts with a wide audience. Viral content can significantly impact the decisions of many traders. For instance, discussions on Reddit forums contributed to the spectacular rise in GameStop's stock.

Currently Most Discussed Stocks:

- Tesla: Tesla's popularity on social media is driven by constant innovation and Elon Musk's charismatic personality. In January 2023, Tesla's stock was at $108.10 and rose to $164.90 by April 2023, marking a 52% increase.

- Apple: Apple has garnered significant interest with 33 million views on TikTok and 19,000 posts on Instagram. Its stock went from $124.22 to $169.58, a 36% increase during the same period.

- Amazon: Highly favored on social media, Amazon's stock surged by 115% in just over a year, with hashtags viewed 13 million times on TikTok.

- Walmart: With 8.9 million views on TikTok, Walmart ranks fourth among the most discussed stocks.

- Meta: Known for its multiple apps and the launch of Threads, Meta saw its stock climb from $124.61 in January 2023 to $527.34 in April 2024, a 323% increase.

- Nvidia: The graphics processor specialist saw significant growth due to the excitement around AI, becoming one of the most traded stocks on the New York Stock Exchange.

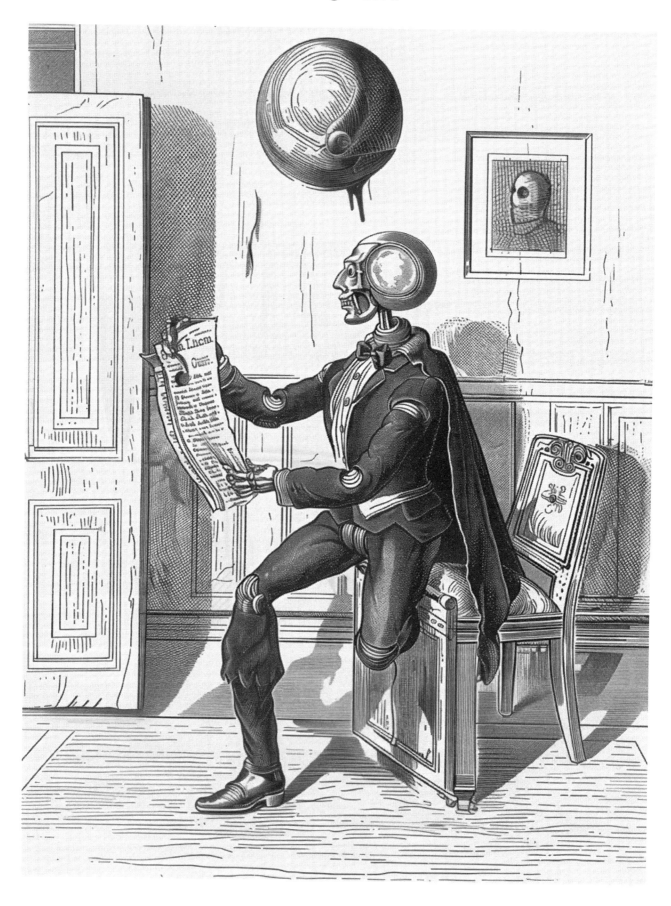

How AI Can Observe Social Media

AI can analyze social media discussions in several ways:

1. Real-Time Data Collection: AI algorithms can continuously monitor thousands of posts, comments, and videos, capturing data on mentioned stocks, user sentiments, and emerging trends.
2. Sentiment Analysis: Using Natural Language Processing (NLP) techniques, AI can determine whether discussions around a stock are positive or negative, providing valuable indicators of potential market movements.
3. Trend Identification: By combining sentiment data with the volume of mentions and the speed of diffusion, AI can identify emerging trends before they become apparent to the broader market.
4. Market Movement Prediction: Machine learning models can correlate social media discussions with historical market movements to predict future trends.

Case Studies and Examples

1. Tesla: Frequent discussions about innovations and Elon Musk's announcements can be analyzed to detect positive or negative sentiment trends, influencing buying or selling decisions.
2. Dogecoin: Sudden and positive mentions on social media have often preceded price surges, a trend that AI can identify and exploit.
3. Amazon: Analyzing social media discussions around high-demand periods, such as Prime Days, can provide insights into short-term price variations.

Advantages and Limitations

Advantages:

- Responsiveness: Real-time data analysis allows for quick reactions to market changes.
- Precision: Provides more accurate insights by processing vast amounts of data.
- Automation: AI can automate trend monitoring, enabling traders to focus on strategy execution.

Limitations:

- Data Quality: Social media data can contain erroneous or misleading information.
- Market Manipulation: Discussions can be influenced by actors seeking to manipulate the market, skewing AI analyses.
- Chain Reactions: Excessive reliance on AI and social media data can cause chain reactions that amplify volatility.

Conclusion

Integrating AI into the analysis of social media discussions offers a new dimension for traders seeking to identify market trends. By monitoring and analyzing conversations on TikTok and Instagram in real-time, AI can provide valuable insights that, when used judiciously, can offer a significant competitive advantage. However, it is crucial to combine these analyses with other data sources and remain vigilant against market manipulation attempts.

Chapter 8:
The Future of AI in Trading

As Martin Luther King would say :

I have a dream that one day, in the world of trading and finance, AI will be used not just as a tool for profit, but as a force for equality, empowerment, and social good. I dream of a future where AI in trading will level the playing field for all traders, regardless of their background or resources, and create opportunities for everyone to succeed.

I have a dream that one day, AI algorithms will not only analyze market data and predict trends, but also promote transparency, fairness, and ethical practices in the financial markets. I dream of a future where AI will help prevent market manipulation, insider trading, and other unethical behaviors, ensuring a more just and equitable trading environment for all.

I have a dream that one day, AI in trading will empower individuals and communities to make informed decisions, manage risks effectively, and achieve financial independence. I dream of a future where AI tools will provide educational resources, training programs, and support networks to help traders of all backgrounds thrive and prosper in the world of finance.

I have a dream that one day, AI will be used not just to maximize profits, but to drive positive social impact and create a more sustainable and inclusive financial system. I dream of a future where AI in trading will be a force for good, promoting responsible investing, supporting sustainable development goals, and fostering economic empowerment for all.

With this dream in our hearts and a vision of a brighter future ahead, let us work together to harness the power of AI in trading for the greater good, to build a more just, equitable, and prosperous world for all.

As Martin Luther King once said, "The time is always right to do what is right." Let us strive towards a future where AI in trading embodies these principles and paves the way for a more inclusive and equitable financial landscape.

Trends in AI Technology for Trading

Anyway if we come back to the recent years, the use of artificial intelligence (AI) technology in trading has become increasingly prevalent, revolutionizing the way non-professional traders approach the financial markets. This subchapter will explore the latest trends in AI technology for trading and how everyday traders can leverage these advancements to enhance their trading strategies.

One of the most significant trends in AI technology for trading is the rise of machine learning algorithms. These algorithms can analyze vast amounts of data and identify patterns that may not be apparent to human traders. By using machine learning models, non-professional traders can make more informed trading decisions and potentially increase their profitability.

Another trend in AI technology for trading is the integration of natural language processing (NLP) tools. These tools can analyze news articles, social media posts, and other sources of information to help traders better understand market sentiment and make more informed decisions. By utilizing NLP technology, non-professional traders can stay ahead of market trends and make more accurate predictions about future price movements.

Additionally, the use of AI-powered trading bots is becoming increasingly popular among non-professional traders. These bots can execute trades on behalf of traders based on pre-defined criteria and algorithms. By using trading bots, non-professional traders can automate their trading strategies and take advantage of market opportunities 24/7.

Overall, the trends in AI technology for trading are rapidly evolving, providing non-professional traders with new tools and resources to improve their trading strategies. By staying informed about the latest advancements in AI technology for trading, everyday traders can stay ahead of the curve and maximize their potential for success in the financial markets.

Ethical Considerations of AI in Trading

In the world of trading, the use of artificial intelligence (AI) has become increasingly popular among both professional and non-professional traders. However, with this powerful technology comes ethical considerations that must be taken into account.

One of the key ethical considerations of AI in trading is the potential for bias in the algorithms used. AI systems are only as good as the data they are trained on, and if that data is biased in any way, it can lead to unfair outcomes. Non-professional traders must be aware of this risk and take steps to ensure that the AI systems they are using are as unbiased as possible.

Another ethical consideration is the potential for AI to be used for market manipulation. As AI systems become more sophisticated, there is a risk that unscrupulous traders could use them to manipulate markets for their own gain. Non-professional traders must be vigilant in ensuring that their AI systems are used ethically and in compliance with market regulations.

Additionally, there is the ethical consideration of transparency in AI trading systems. Non-professional traders must be able to understand how their AI systems are making decisions and be able to explain those decisions to others. This transparency is essential for building trust in AI systems and ensuring that they are being used responsibly.

Overall, non-professional traders must be mindful of the ethical considerations of AI in trading and take steps to ensure that they are using this technology in a responsible and ethical manner. By being aware of potential biases, avoiding market manipulation, and promoting transparency, non-professional traders can harness the power of AI in their trading strategies while upholding ethical standards.

Opportunities for Non-Professional Traders in the AI Trading Space

As a non-professional trader, you may feel overwhelmed by the complexities of the financial markets and the fast-paced nature of trading. However, with the rise of artificial intelligence (AI) technology, there are now more opportunities than ever for traders like you to succeed in the market.

One of the key opportunities for non-professional traders in the AI trading space is the ability to access sophisticated trading algorithms and data analytics tools that were once only available to large financial institutions. These AI-powered tools can help you make more informed trading decisions by analyzing vast amounts of market data in real-time and identifying profitable trading opportunities.

Additionally, AI trading systems can help you automate your trading strategies, allowing you to execute trades more efficiently and effectively. This can help you take advantage of market opportunities as they arise, without having to constantly monitor the markets yourself.

Another opportunity for non-professional traders in the AI trading space is the ability to leverage machine learning algorithms to improve their trading performance over time. By analyzing your trading data and identifying patterns and trends, AI systems can help you refine your trading strategies and make better decisions in the future.

Overall, the opportunities for non-professional traders in the AI trading space are vast and can help level the playing field between individual traders and institutional investors. By leveraging AI technology in your trading strategy, you can increase your chances of success in the market and achieve your financial goals.

Clubs of people trading and using AI signals

There are communities and clubs of traders who use AI signals and algorithms to inform their trading decisions. These groups often gather online or in person to exchange ideas, share strategies, and collaborate on using AI technologies to enhance their trading performance. Here are a few examples of such communities:

- **Quantitative Trading Groups** : Quantitative trading groups are communities of traders and investors who use quantitative methods, including AI and machine learning algorithms, to analyze market data and develop trading strategies. These groups often share research, tools, and insights related to algorithmic trading and quantitative analysis.

- **Algorithmic Trading Societies** : Algorithmic trading societies are organizations that bring together traders and professionals interested in algorithmic trading and automated investing. These societies host events, workshops, and networking opportunities for members to learn about the latest developments in AI trading technologies.

- **Online Trading Forums** : There are online trading forums and communities where traders discuss AI signals, trading algorithms, and automated trading strategies. Platforms such as Reddit, TradingView, and QuantConnect's community forum are popular spaces for traders to share AI signals and collaborate on trading ideas.

- **AI Trading Platforms** : Some AI trading platforms offer community features that allow traders to connect with other users, share AI signals, and collaborate on trading strategies. These platforms provide a social trading environment where traders can follow and copy the trades of successful AI-powered strategies.

A few other examples

The Quant Club

The Quant Club is a group dedicated to quantitative traders and computational finance enthusiasts. The club organizes events, seminars and knowledge-sharing sessions to help members improve their quantitative trading skills.

Reddit Trading Groups

Groups like r/quantfinance and r/algotrading on Reddit are also active communities where traders share strategies, discuss AI algorithms and exchange algorithmic trading tips.

Renaissance Technologies

Renaissance Technologies is one of the most famous algorithmic trading companies, founded by James Simons. Their flagship fund, Medallion Fund, uses complex mathematical models and algorithms to analyze and trade the financial markets, and has generated exceptional returns over the years.

Two Sigma

Two Sigma is a technology-based fund management company that uses machine learning techniques, data analysis and algorithms to develop trading strategies. It manages billions of dollars in assets and stands out for its scientific approach to trading.

DE Shaw

DE Shaw is an investment fund management company that combines expertise in finance and technology to develop algorithmic trading strategies. The company is known for its advanced use of AI and quantitative techniques to analyze markets.

Citadel

Citadel is another leading algorithmic trading company, headed by Kenneth Griffin. It uses mathematical models and algorithms to perform high-frequency trades and manage a diversified portfolio of financial assets.

AQR Capital Management

AQR Capital Management is a fund management company that integrates academic research and quantitative models into its trading strategies. AQR uses advanced quantitative techniques to exploit market inefficiencies and generate returns for its investors.

By joining these communities and clubs, traders can access valuable resources, insights, and support from like-minded individuals who are also using AI signals and algorithms in their trading activities. Collaborating with others in these groups can help traders stay informed about the latest trends in AI trading, learn from each other's experiences, and improve their trading performance using AI technologies.

Chapter 9:
Key Takeaways for Non-Professional Traders

As a non-professional trader looking to incorporate artificial intelligence into your trading strategy, there are several key takeaways that you should keep in mind. By understanding these key points, you can maximize the benefits of using AI in your trading and improve your overall success in the market.

First and foremost, it is essential to recognize that AI is a powerful tool that can help you make more informed trading decisions. By leveraging AI algorithms and machine learning models, you can analyze vast amounts of data and identify patterns that may not be apparent to the human eye. This can give you a significant edge in the market and help you make more profitable trades.

Additionally, it is crucial to understand that AI is not a magic bullet that will guarantee success in trading. While AI can provide valuable insights and help you make better decisions, it is still important to combine AI with your own knowledge and expertise. By using AI as a supplement to your trading strategy, rather than a replacement for it, you can maximize its benefits and improve your overall performance.

Furthermore, it is important to continuously monitor and adjust your AI-based trading strategy. The market is constantly evolving, and what works today may not work tomorrow. By regularly evaluating the performance of your AI models and making necessary adjustments, you can ensure that your trading strategy remains effective and profitable.

In conclusion, non-professional traders can benefit greatly from incorporating AI into their trading strategy. By understanding the key takeaways outlined in this subchapter and applying them to your own trading practices, you can harness the power of AI to improve your trading performance and achieve greater success in the market.

Thoughts on Embracing AI in Your Trading Strategy

In conclusion, incorporating artificial intelligence into your trading strategy can be a game-changer for non-professional traders looking to make more informed and profitable decisions in the market. By leveraging the power of AI tools and algorithms, you can gain a competitive edge and stay ahead of the curve in the fast-paced world of trading.

One of the key takeaways from this book is the importance of understanding how AI works and how it can be applied to your unique trading style. By taking the time to learn about different AI technologies and their potential applications, you can make more educated decisions about which tools are best suited for your needs.

Additionally, it's crucial to remember that while AI can provide valuable insights and analysis, it should not be relied upon as the sole basis for your trading decisions. Human intuition and experience still play a vital role in successful trading, so it's essential to use AI as a complementary tool rather than a replacement for traditional methods.

As you continue to explore the world of trading with AI, don't be afraid to experiment and try new strategies. Keep an open mind and be willing to adapt your approach based on the feedback and results you receive. With time and practice, you can refine your trading strategy and achieve your financial goals with the help of artificial intelligence.

In conclusion, embracing AI in your trading strategy can revolutionize the way you approach the market and help you achieve greater success as a non-professional trader. By staying informed, open-minded, and willing to learn, you can harness the power of AI to take your trading to the next level.

But don't forget that Warren Buffett emphasizes the importance of patience and discipline in investing.

"The stock market is designed to transfer money from the Active to the Patient." - Warren Buffett

Investing requires a long-term perspective, discipline, and the ability to resist the temptation to constantly trade or speculate in the market. He encourages individuals to focus on fundamental analysis, value investing principles, and staying committed to their investment strategies over time.

IA can definitely helps you for that. Good Luck !!!

Chapter 10 : Leveraging ChatGPT for Enhanced Trading Strategies

Introduction to ChatGPT

What is ChatGPT?

ChatGPT is indeed a specialized iteration of the Generative Pretrained Transformer (GPT) models developed by OpenAI. These models are fundamentally designed to understand and generate text that closely mimics human conversation. Here's a breakdown of how ChatGPT applies its capabilities in the context of trading and financial analysis:

1. Interpreting Market News: ChatGPT can quickly digest and summarize financial news, helping traders and investors stay updated with the latest market trends and significant events. It can process vast amounts of textual information, from news articles and analyst reports to social media feeds, providing condensed and relevant insights.
2. Analyzing Financial Reports: By leveraging its trained ability on a diverse range of texts, including complex financial documents, ChatGPT can assist in interpreting quarterly reports, SEC filings, and earnings releases. It can highlight key financial metrics and performance indicators, making it easier for users to gauge a company's financial health without delving into the intricate details of full reports.
3. Engaging in Informative Dialogues: ChatGPT can participate in conversations about stock trends and trading strategies. It can provide explanations on basic and advanced trading concepts, discuss historical market performance, and explore hypothetical trading scenarios based on historical data.

While ChatGPT is adept at processing and generating text-based information, it's important to note that it doesn't have real-time access to market data and should not be used as the sole tool for making financial decisions. It works best when used in conjunction with professional financial advice and up-to-date market analysis.

As we have seen earlier, Natural Language Processing (NLP) is a branch of artificial intelligence that focuses on the interaction between computers and humans through natural language. The goal of NLP is to enable computers to understand, interpret, and produce human language in a way that is both valuable and meaningful.

Here's how it works and how ChatGPT leverages this technology:

How ChatGPT Uses NLP

1. Understanding Text: ChatGPT processes input text by breaking it down into understandable segments. It analyzes the structure and meaning of the text, using models trained on vast datasets to grasp context, sentiment, and intent.
2. Generating Text: Based on the analysis of the input text, ChatGPT generates responses that are coherent and contextually relevant. It uses patterns learned during training to construct sentences, maintaining a natural flow that mirrors human conversation.
3. Learning from Context: NLP enables ChatGPT to consider the wider context of a conversation. This means it can maintain topic relevance over the course of an interaction and adjust its responses according to the nuances of the dialogue.

Relevance to Trading

In the trading and financial domain, NLP can be particularly transformative:

1. Sentiment Analysis: NLP can analyze news articles, social media posts, and analyst reports to determine the sentiment around certain stocks or the market overall. This helps in predicting market trends based on the emotions and opinions expressed in large volumes of text.
2. Automated Reporting: Traders can use NLP to automatically generate summaries of financial documents, earning reports, and the latest market news, saving time and providing insights at a glance.
3. Real-Time Communications: NLP enables real-time, automated communication with market participants. Chatbots equipped with NLP can handle inquiries about market conditions, stock performance, and trading strategies, offering rapid responses that are informed by historical data and market trends.
4. Complex Query Understanding: Traders can ask complex questions about market data, financial forecasts, and investment opportunities. NLP helps in parsing these queries and providing detailed, contextual answers that can aid decision-making.

By integrating NLP, trading platforms can enhance their interface between users and the vast amounts of data they handle daily, making it more interactive, responsive, and user-friendly. While ChatGPT itself is not a trading tool, its underlying NLP capabilities make it an excellent partner for applications that require sophisticated text analysis and interaction within the financial sector.

The role of AI, particularly through tools like ChatGPT, in financial analysis has been expanding, emphasizing its potential to enhance non-technical aspects of trading. This integration caters to enhancing customer experience, simplifying complex data interpretation, and providing support for decision-making in trading. Here's how ChatGPT, with its AI-driven capabilities, can assist in various trading-related tasks:

Non-Technical Applications of ChatGPT in Trading

1. Customer Support and Interaction: ChatGPT can serve as a first point of contact for traders and investors on trading platforms. It can handle inquiries about account information, trading guidelines, transaction processes, and more, providing instant responses and reducing wait times for human support.
2. Educational Tool: For beginners and seasoned traders alike, ChatGPT can explain trading concepts, from basic terms like stocks, bonds, and mutual funds to more complex ideas such as options strategies, futures contracts, and technical analysis. This educational support is crucial for making informed trading decisions.
3. Market Summaries: ChatGPT can provide daily or weekly market summaries based on the latest news and reports. By synthesizing information from multiple sources, it can highlight key events that could influence the market, offering traders a quick overview without needing to review extensive documentation themselves.
4. Risk Communication: It can communicate potential risks involved in trading certain instruments or adopting specific strategies. By understanding the user's context through questions or expressed concerns, ChatGPT can provide tailored advice, including warnings about volatile investments or the implications of economic changes.

Examples of Trading-Related Tasks for ChatGPT

Here are specific examples of questions and tasks that ChatGPT can assist with in a trading context:

Query: *"Can you explain what a dividend is and which companies have announced dividend increases?"*
Task: ChatGPT can explain the concept of dividends and generate a summary of recent news articles about companies that have announced dividend increases.

Query: *"What are the implications of the Federal Reserve's latest interest rate decision?"*
Task: ChatGPT can provide a simplified explanation of the Federal Reserve's decisions on interest rates and discuss potential impacts on different sectors of the market.

Query: *"Can you provide a summary of Tesla's latest earnings report?"*
Task: ChatGPT can summarize key points from Tesla's latest earnings report, focusing on net income, revenue changes, and forward-looking statements made by the company's management.

Query: *"How do I start trading options, and what are the risks involved?"*
Task: ChatGPT can outline steps to start trading options, explain basic strategies, and discuss associated risks, helping users understand both the potential benefits and downsides.

Query: *"What are the current trends in the cryptocurrency market?"*
 Task: Although it doesn't have real-time data, ChatGPT can discuss recent trends and major news affecting the cryptocurrency market based on the latest available information.

Through these tasks, ChatGPT helps bridge the gap between complex financial data and user-friendly information, making trading more accessible to a wider audience. This non-technical support is crucial for many users who may not have a deep financial background but wish to participate actively in trading.

Getting Started with ChatGPT for Trading

So let's see how to Access ChatGPT.

1. OpenAI Website

The most straightforward method is to use ChatGPT directly through OpenAI's website:

- Step 1: Visit <u>OpenAI's ChatGPT page</u>.

- Step 2: Sign up or log in if you already have an account.

- Step 3: Start interacting with ChatGPT by typing your questions or prompts related to trading.

2. Third-Party Trading Platforms with AI Integration

Several trading platforms have begun integrating AI technologies, including capabilities similar to ChatGPT, to enhance user experience, provide real-time analytics, and offer automated customer support. Here are a few notable examples:

A. Interactive Brokers

- AI Features: Interactive Brokers uses AI to provide natural language processing capabilities, allowing users to type commands and queries in plain English directly into the trading interface.

- Applications: Users can ask about stock prices, get account updates, or even execute trades using natural language commands.
-

B. E*TRADE

- AI Features: E*TRADE has integrated an AI-driven assistant that helps users navigate the platform and provides answers to common questions about trading and personal accounts.

- Applications: The AI assistant can help with retrieving market data, understanding complex trading terms, and managing transactions.

C. TD Ameritrade

- AI Features: TD Ameritrade offers an AI chatbot named "Ask Ted," which is designed to provide quick answers to customer queries and guide users through the platform's features.

- Applications: Ask Ted can assist with analytical insights, account management tasks, and detailed trading queries.

D. Robinhood

- AI Features: Robinhood uses machine learning models to personalize financial news, notifications, and investment suggestions.
- Applications: The AI helps tailor content to the individual's trading behavior and preferences, enhancing decision-making processes.

E. Saxo Bank

- AI Features: Saxo Bank utilizes AI for both customer service and operational efficiency, including tools that automate trading strategies.
- Applications: Its AI capabilities are used to analyze market trends and help traders develop more informed trading strategies through predictive analytics.

These platforms are examples of how AI is being utilized in the trading sector to improve efficiency, user experience, and accessibility. The integration of AI tools like ChatGPT helps simplify complex trading decisions by providing quick access to information and automating routine tasks. This trend is likely to grow as AI technology advances and becomes more deeply integrated into the financial services industry.

Using ChatGPT for Market Analysis

Analyzing Market News

Using ChatGPT to obtain summaries of financial news can be highly effective for staying updated on specific markets or stocks. Here's a step-by-step guide on how you might use ChatGPT to achieve this, focusing on relevancy and precision:

Step 1: Access ChatGPT

First, access ChatGPT through any of the platforms that support it, such as the OpenAI website, integrated trading platforms, or mobile apps. Ensure you're logged in if necessary.

Step 2: Specify Your Query

Be clear and specific about what you're looking for. The more specific your question, the more relevant the information provided by ChatGPT will be. For example:

- *"Can you provide a summary of today's financial news focusing on the technology sector?"*

- *"I need a summary of recent developments concerning Tesla's stock."*

Step 3: Ask for Additional Details or Clarifications

Once you receive the initial summary, you might find that you need more details or clarification on certain points. Follow up with specific questions to dig deeper:

- *"Can you explain more about the impact of the new government policy on Tesla's stock?"*

- *"What are the key factors driving the current trends in the technology sector?"*

Step 4: Request Comparative Analyses or Historical Context

To understand the significance of the news better, you might want to see it in a broader context:

- *"How does today's performance of the tech sector compare to last month?"*

- *"What has been the trend for Tesla's stock prices following previous earnings announcements?"*

Step 5: Apply the Information

Use the summarized information to make informed decisions or to further your research. If necessary, combine the insights gained from ChatGPT with other sources or tools for a more comprehensive view.

Step 6: Continuous Monitoring

Set up regular prompts to stay updated:

- *"Give me daily updates on news related to Apple's stock."*

- *"Alert me to any major news about changes in cryptocurrency regulations."*

Example Interaction:

User: *"Can you provide a summary of the most important news from the financial markets today, focusing specifically on the healthcare sector?"*

ChatGPT: "Today in the healthcare sector, XYZ Biotech surged 15% after announcing successful Phase 3 trial results for their new drug. Meanwhile, ABC Pharma faced a 5% drop after a recall of one of their leading products due to compliance issues. Lastly, the healthcare sector is seeing increased investor interest following new healthcare reforms announced by the government."

This approach with ChatGPT helps you sift through large amounts of data quickly, focusing only on what's relevant to your interests or investments. By refining your questions and utilizing follow-up queries, you can effectively use ChatGPT to enhance your understanding and stay informed about the financial markets.

Another example on how to use ChatGPT to obtain summaries of financial news, focusing on relevancy to specific markets or stocks.

Prompt: *"What are the key points from today's news about the Federal Reserve's interest rate decision?"*

Understanding Economic Reports

Economic reports can often be dense and packed with complex data, which makes them challenging for traders to quickly understand and use. Here's how you can use ChatGPT to simplify these reports into actionable trading insights:

Step 1: Access ChatGPT

First, ensure you have access to ChatGPT through a compatible platform, whether it's directly through OpenAI's website, a trading platform that integrates AI, or a dedicated app.

Step 2: Input the Economic Report

When you have a specific economic report in mind (e.g., GDP growth figures, unemployment rates, inflation data), you can start by asking ChatGPT to explain the significance of the report. For instance:

- *"Can you explain the latest GDP report and its implications for the stock market?"*

- *"Summarize the key points of the recent consumer price index (CPI) report and how it might affect interest rates."*

Step 3: Ask for Simplification and Clarification

If the initial explanation is still too complex or you need specific parts of the report broken down, ask for simplification:

- *"Can you break down what the changes in the CPI indicate for consumer spending?"*

- *"Explain the term 'non-farm payrolls' in the context of the unemployment report."*

Step 4: Request Insights and Implications

To make the data actionable, ask ChatGPT to translate these economic indicators into potential market movements or trading strategies:

- *"What could be the potential market reaction to this unexpected rise in unemployment rates?"*

- *"How might the latest inflation data influence the Federal Reserve's decisions on interest rates, and what does this mean for my bond investments?"*

Step 5: Comparative Analysis and Trends

Understanding economic data often requires a historical perspective or comparison with market expectations:

- *"Compare the current GDP growth rate with the past quarter and its impact on the S&P 500 index."*

- *"How does this inflation rate compare to the same period last year, and what were the market reactions then?"*

Step 6: Continuous Updates

Since economic conditions evolve, it's useful to set up ongoing inquiries:

- *"Keep me updated on major changes in economic indicators that could impact the automotive sector."*

- *"Alert me to new economic reports related to the real estate market."*

Example Interaction:

User: *"I have the Federal Reserve's latest report on interest rates. Can you help me understand its implications for currency trading?"*

ChatGPT: "Certainly! The Federal Reserve has decided to increase interest rates by 0.25%. This is typically bullish for the USD as higher interest rates can attract foreign capital looking for better returns. You might see strengthening in the USD against other major currencies. It would be wise to monitor currency pairs like EUR/USD or USD/JPY for potential opportunities to capitalize on this trend."

Using ChatGPT in this manner allows you to transform complex economic data into understandable, actionable insights that can inform your trading strategies. By continually engaging with AI in this way, you can maintain an edge in adapting to economic trends and market movements.

Enhancing Trading Decisions with ChatGPT

Trade Idea Generation

- Here we will see how ChatGPT can help generate trading ideas by analyzing current market data and historical trends.

- Prompt: *"Based on the latest market trends, what sectors should I consider investing in this quarter?"*

Enhancing trading decisions with ChatGPT, particularly in the domain of trade idea generation, involves leveraging its capabilities to analyze current market data and historical trends. This process can provide traders with valuable insights and actionable trading ideas. Here's how ChatGPT can be effectively used for generating trade ideas:

Understanding Trade Idea Generation with ChatGPT

1. Data Analysis Capability:

ChatGPT can be employed to analyze vast amounts of data quickly. While the model itself doesn't directly process raw market data or perform quantitative analysis, it can interpret the results from such analyses that are fed into it in a textual format. This allows traders to ask questions about data analyses and receive interpretations in an understandable form.

2. Historical Trend Analysis:

Traders can discuss historical market trends and their implications with ChatGPT.

For example, by providing summaries or insights from existing financial reports or data analysis outputs, traders can ask ChatGPT to compare these trends against current market conditions. This can help in identifying patterns that are likely to repeat or in forecasting future market behavior.

3. Scenario Simulation:

ChatGPT can assist in simulating different trading scenarios based on historical data. Traders can ask hypothetical questions like, "What might happen to tech stocks if the interest rates increase by 1%?" ChatGPT can use available historical data insights to craft responses that might indicate possible market reactions based on similar past events.

Practical Steps for Using ChatGPT in Trade Idea Generation

Step 1: Query Preparation

Prepare specific queries related to market trends, economic indicators, or specific stocks. The clearer and more precise the questions, the better the quality of the responses from ChatGPT.

Step 2: Input Interpretation

Present your data analysis findings or market summaries to ChatGPT in a clear format. For example, "Based on the last quarter's data, tech stocks have shown a 5% growth rate in a bullish market. How would potential regulatory changes impact this trend?"

Step 3: Analyzing Responses

Analyze the responses from ChatGPT for insights into market dynamics or potential investment opportunities. ChatGPT might provide perspectives on how certain trends could evolve, offering a foundation for trade idea generation.

Step 4: Continuous Feedback Loop
Use a feedback loop where the outcomes of predicted trends are discussed again with

ChatGPT to refine future queries and improve understanding. This iterative process helps in sharpening the trade ideas over time.

Example of Generating Trade Ideas Using ChatGPT

Example Query:

"Given the historical resilience of utility stocks during economic downturns, how might an impending recession impact sectors like technology and consumer discretionary?"

ChatGPT's Response:

"In previous recessions, utility stocks have indeed shown resilience, often outperforming the market. For sectors like technology and consumer discretionary, a recession could lead to reduced consumer spending and lower earnings. However, certain technology sub-sectors, such as cloud computing and cybersecurity, may continue to grow due to ongoing digital transformation needs."

Application:

This insight can help a trader decide to reallocate investments, potentially increasing holdings in utility stocks while being more selective within the technology sector, focusing on sub-sectors likely to maintain growth.

Using ChatGPT for trade idea generation involves leveraging its natural language processing strengths to interpret data and trends, simulate scenarios, and generate actionable trading insights. By integrating ChatGPT into their analysis workflow, traders can enhance decision-making processes, uncover new trading opportunities, and refine their strategies with a better understanding of complex market dynamics.

Strategy Discussion

- ChatGPT can help evaluate different trading strategies based on current market conditions.

- Prompt: *"Compare the effectiveness of short selling vs. long-term investment strategies in the current economic environment."*

Risk Management with ChatGPT

Risk management is crucial in trading, and utilizing ChatGPT to identify and analyze potential risks can significantly enhance decision-making. Here are some examples showing how traders might use ChatGPT to discuss and evaluate risks associated with their trading portfolios.

Example 1: Portfolio Overexposure to a Single Sector

Trader: *"I've noticed a large portion of my portfolio is concentrated in the tech sector. What are the potential risks?"*

ChatGPT: "Concentrating a large portion of your portfolio in a single sector, such as technology, exposes you to sector-specific risks. These can include regulatory changes, technological disruptions, or shifts in consumer preferences that disproportionately affect tech companies. Economic factors like interest rate hikes can also impact growth-oriented sectors like tech more significantly than others. This overexposure can lead to higher volatility and potential losses if the sector faces a downturn."

Trader: *"How can I mitigate this risk?"*

ChatGPT: "To mitigate the risk of overexposure, consider diversifying your portfolio across multiple sectors. This might involve reallocating some of your investments from technology to more stable sectors such as utilities or consumer staples, which are less sensitive to economic cycles. Additionally, regularly reviewing your portfolio's sector allocation can help you maintain a balanced exposure, reducing potential risks and smoothing out returns over time."

Example 2: Risks from High Leverage

Trader: *"I am using leverage to enhance my trading returns. What should I be aware of?"*

ChatGPT: "Using leverage can significantly increase your potential returns, but it also amplifies your risks. If the market moves against your position, leverage can lead to large losses relative to your initial investment. Additionally, there is the risk of a margin call if your account balance falls below the broker's required level, which could force you to liquidate positions at unfavorable prices."

Trader: *"What strategies can I use to manage leverage risk?"*

ChatGPT: "To manage leverage risk effectively, consider implementing strict risk management rules. Set a cap on the total amount of leverage you use relative to your portfolio value. Use stop-loss orders to automatically close positions at a predetermined price level, limiting your losses. Also, continuously monitor the market conditions and adjust your leverage usage based on the level of volatility and market liquidity. Lastly, maintain a sufficient cash buffer in your account to handle margin calls without needing to liquidate positions hastily."

Example 3: Risk of Significant Market Events

Trader: *"How can I prepare my portfolio for unexpected market events like a financial crisis?"*

ChatGPT: "Preparing for significant market events involves building resilience into your portfolio. One strategy is to include asset classes that are historically known to be less correlated or even inversely correlated with the market, such as gold or certain fixed-income securities. Also, consider maintaining a portion of your portfolio in cash or cash equivalents to take advantage of new opportunities as they arise during a downturn."

Trader: *"Is there a way to predict these events?"*

ChatGPT: "While predicting the exact timing of market crises is challenging, you can monitor economic indicators and market sentiment for potential warning signs. Keep an eye on high levels of market leverage, unusual fluctuations in commodity prices, and significant shifts in government policies or interest rates. Tools like economic calendars, financial news aggregators, and predictive analytics using AI can help you stay informed and react more swiftly to emerging risks."

These examples demonstrate how ChatGPT can help traders analyze different types of risks in their portfolios and discuss strategies to mitigate those risks effectively. By engaging in such dialogues, traders can make more informed decisions and maintain a healthier risk profile in their trading activities.

- Finally, ChatGPT can help to identify and analyze potential risks in a trading portfolio.

- Prompt: *"Analyze the risk of investing in high-yield bonds in the current interest rate climate."*

Compliance and Regulations

- Utilizing ChatGPT to keep up-to-date with the latest trading regulations and compliance requirements.

- Prompt: *"Summarize the latest FINRA regulations affecting cryptocurrency trading."*

Staying compliant with trading regulations and understanding the latest requirements are critical for traders to avoid legal pitfalls and manage risk effectively. ChatGPT can be an invaluable resource for summarizing complex regulatory documents, providing updates on new regulations, and explaining how these changes might impact trading activities. Here are some examples of how traders can use ChatGPT to stay informed about compliance and regulations:

Example 1: Understanding New Regulatory Changes

Trader: *"Can you explain the latest SEC amendments to Rule 10b5-1 and how they might affect my trading plans?"*

ChatGPT: "The latest amendments to SEC Rule 10b5-1 involve stricter requirements for corporate insiders to prevent illegal insider trading. Key changes include:

1. Cooling-off Period: Insiders must now wait a mandatory cooling-off period after adopting a 10b5-1 plan before they can start trading. For company directors and officers, the cooling-off period is six months, and for other employees, it is three months.

2. Certifications: When adopting a 10b5-1 plan, insiders must certify that they are not in possession of material non-public information (MNPI).

3. Limit on Multiple Plans: The amendments restrict the ability to maintain multiple, overlapping 10b5-1 plans.

These changes are designed to enhance transparency and prevent abuses of the rule, which could impact your trading plans if you're considered an insider or if your trades might be influenced by insiders' actions."

Trader: *"How should I adjust my trading strategy in response to this?"*

ChatGPT: "To align with the new amendments, ensure that any 10b5-1 trading plans you're part of fully comply with the new cooling-off periods and certification requirements. Consider consulting with a compliance officer or legal advisor to review your trading strategies and ensure they adhere to these updated regulations. It's also beneficial to implement robust monitoring systems to keep track of any trades made under these plans to ensure ongoing compliance."

Example 2: Staying Updated on Global Trading Regulations

Trader: *"I trade on multiple international exchanges. How can I keep up with regulatory changes across different markets?"*

ChatGPT: "Managing compliance in multiple international markets requires a proactive approach:

1. Regular Updates: Subscribe to regulatory news feeds or use a compliance monitoring service that alerts you to regulatory changes in the markets where you are active.

2. Local Legal Counsel: Work with legal advisors in each jurisdiction to understand localized regulatory requirements and receive timely updates on changes.

3. Compliance Software: Consider investing in compliance management software that can help you track and adapt to regulatory changes across different regions.

Example 3: Understanding Cryptocurrency Regulations

Trader: *"What are the current regulatory considerations for trading cryptocurrencies in the U.S.?"*

ChatGPT: "Cryptocurrency trading in the U.S. is primarily overseen by the SEC and CFTC, and it's subject to a rapidly evolving regulatory landscape. Key considerations include:

1. Securities Law: Depending on how they are issued and traded, some cryptocurrencies might be classified as securities and thus subject to SEC regulations.

2. Anti-Money Laundering (AML): Cryptocurrency exchanges must comply with AML regulations under the Bank Secrecy Act, requiring KYC (Know Your Customer) processes.

3. Tax Obligations: The IRS requires reporting of gains and losses from cryptocurrency transactions, similar to other capital assets.

It's important to regularly review guidelines issued by these regulatory bodies and consider legal consultation to ensure compliance with the current laws."

These examples illustrate how ChatGPT can assist traders in navigating the complex world of financial regulations by providing clear explanations of regulatory requirements, suggesting ways to stay updated, and helping traders understand the implications of these regulations on their trading strategies.

Practical Examples and Case Studies

Case Study 1: Market Downturn

We will see a detailed scenario on how ChatGPT could be used to adapt trading strategies during a market downturn. And how ChatGPT's insights could lead to strategic adjustments, minimizing losses and capitalizing on market recoveries.

Scenario: Adapting Trading Strategies During a Market Downturn Using ChatGPT

Background

Market downturns can be challenging for traders, often marked by increased volatility and a general decline in stock prices. Traders need to swiftly adapt their strategies to mitigate losses and position themselves for potential recovery. Here, we explore how ChatGPT can be instrumental during such times.

Initial Situation

Imagine a trader, Alex, who has a diversified portfolio primarily composed of tech stocks, which are particularly vulnerable during the downturn due to high valuation levels. As the market begins to decline, Alex turns to ChatGPT for assistance in navigating the challenging environment.

Step 1: Immediate Assessment of Market Conditions

Alex: *"Can you provide an analysis of the current market conditions and how they are impacting tech stocks?"*

ChatGPT: "The current market downturn appears to be driven by a combination of rising interest rates and slowing economic growth, which are prompting investors to move away from growth-oriented tech stocks due to their high valuations and risk profiles. The tech sector has seen a significant sell-off, with major indices reflecting a downward trend of approximately 10% this quarter. Volatility is high, indicating uncertain investor sentiment."

Step 2: Strategy Adjustment Suggestions

Alex: *"Given these conditions, what strategies would you recommend to mitigate risks?"*

ChatGPT: "In the current volatile market, consider the following strategic adjustments:

1. Rebalance Portfolio: Reduce exposure to high-growth tech stocks and increase holdings in more defensive sectors like utilities or consumer staples, which tend to perform better during downturns.

2. Hedging: Implement hedging strategies using options, such as buying put options to protect against further declines in your most vulnerable positions.

3. Dollar-Cost Averaging: If you believe in the long-term potential of your holdings, consider dollar-cost averaging to reduce the impact of volatility.

4. Stop-Loss Orders: Set stop-loss orders to automatically sell off assets that reach a predetermined price threshold to prevent significant losses."

Step 3: Seeking Opportunities for Recovery

Alex: *"How can I prepare to capitalize on a market recovery?"*

ChatGPT: "To position yourself for recovery, focus on:

1. Quality Stocks: Look for high-quality stocks that have been oversold but have strong fundamentals, solid earnings, and good market positions.

2. Sector Rotation: Monitor sectors that typically rebound early from downturns, such as consumer discretionary or industrial sectors.

3. Liquidity Management: Maintain sufficient liquidity to take advantage of new investment opportunities as the market begins to recover.

4. Stay Informed: Keep abreast of economic indicators and market sentiment shifts that may signal the beginning of a recovery phase."

Step 4: Continuous Monitoring and Adjustment

Alex: *"How should I monitor my portfolio and adjust my strategy moving forward?"*

ChatGPT: "Continuously monitor the following:

1. Economic Indicators: Keep an eye on interest rates, employment data, and GDP growth rates, as these can impact market conditions and investor sentiment.

2. Market Trends: Use technical analysis to watch for trends in stock prices and market indices, looking for signs of stabilization or recovery.

3. Portfolio Performance: Regularly review your portfolio's performance against benchmarks and adjust your strategy accordingly.

4. Stay Flexible: Be ready to adapt your strategy based on new information or changes in market conditions to mitigate risks and seize emerging opportunities."

By leveraging ChatGPT during a market downturn, Alex can make informed decisions quickly, adapting his trading strategy to minimize losses and position for potential market recovery. ChatGPT's ability to analyze vast amounts of data and provide strategic recommendations allows Alex to navigate the downturn more effectively, maintaining a proactive and informed trading approach.

Case Study 2: Economic Indicators

How to leverage economic indicators to forecast market movements using ChatGPT.

Leveraging Economic Indicators to Forecast Market Movements Using ChatGPT

Scenario: Predicting Stock Market Responses to Changes in Consumer Confidence Indices

Economic indicators are vital tools for investors and traders to gauge the health of the economy and predict future market movements. Consumer confidence indices, in particular, can provide insights into consumer sentiment, which is a significant driver of economic activity. In this scenario, we'll explore how a trader, named Jordan, uses ChatGPT to understand and predict how changes in consumer confidence might impact the stock market.

Step 1: Understanding the Economic Indicator

Jordan: *"Can you explain what the consumer confidence index is and why it's important for the stock market?"*

ChatGPT: "The consumer confidence index measures how optimistic or pessimistic consumers are regarding their expected financial situation. This index is a key indicator of the overall health of the economy because consumer spending drives a significant portion of economic activity. A high consumer confidence index suggests that consumers are willing to spend more, which can lead to higher sales and profits for companies, typically leading to stock market gains. Conversely, a low confidence index might indicate reduced spending, potentially hurting corporate profits and negatively impacting the stock market."

Step 2: Analyzing Recent Data

Jordan: *"The latest report shows a sharp decline in consumer confidence from the previous month. How might this affect the stock market?"*

ChatGPT: "A sharp decline in consumer confidence can be a precursor to decreased consumer spending, which could lead to lower sales revenues for publicly traded companies. This is particularly impactful on sectors reliant on discretionary spending, such as retail, luxury goods, and consumer services. Stocks in these sectors might experience declines following such a report. Additionally, a significant drop in consumer confidence could lead to broader market instability as investors anticipate potential downturns in economic growth and adjust their portfolios accordingly."

Step 3: Predicting Sectoral Impact

Jordan: *"Which sectors are likely to be most affected by this drop in consumer confidence?"*

ChatGPT: "Sectors that are highly sensitive to consumer spending patterns are likely to be most affected. These include:

- Retail: Especially companies focusing on non-essential goods.
- Automotive: As consumers might delay big-ticket purchases like cars.
- Consumer Durables: Including electronics and appliances, which are often optional purchases.

Hospitality and Leisure: Such as hotels, restaurants, and entertainment services.

On the other hand, essential services like utilities, healthcare, and basic consumer staples may see less impact as spending on these items is less discretionary."

Step 4: Strategic Investment Decisions

Jordan: *"Given this information, how should I adjust my portfolio?"*

ChatGPT: "Considering the expected impact on consumer spending, you might consider:

1. Reducing Exposure: Lighten holdings in sectors likely to be negatively affected by the drop in consumer confidence.

2. Defensive Positioning: Increase investments in defensive sectors like utilities, healthcare, and consumer staples, which tend to be more resilient during economic downturns.

3. Opportunistic Buys: Look for undervalued opportunities in affected sectors that may rebound quickly once consumer confidence restores.

4. Diversification: Ensure your portfolio is well-diversified across sectors and geographies to mitigate potential losses."

Step 5: Continuous Monitoring and Adjustment

Jordan: *"How often should I review these indicators and my portfolio strategy?"*

ChatGPT: "Economic indicators like the consumer confidence index are typically released monthly. It's a good practice to review these releases regularly and assess their potential impact on your portfolio. Additionally, keep an eye on related economic news, market trends, and other indicators such as employment rates and GDP growth, which can provide further context to changes in consumer sentiment. Adjust your investment strategy based on this analysis and the overall economic outlook."

By leveraging ChatGPT, Jordan can gain a deeper understanding of economic indicators such as the consumer confidence index and their potential impact on the stock market. This scenario illustrates how traders can use ChatGPT to aid in interpreting complex economic data and making informed strategic decisions to optimize their investment portfolios in response to changing market conditions.

Advanced Tips for Using ChatGPT

Crafting effective prompts is crucial when interacting with ChatGPT, especially in trading where the precision of information can significantly impact decision-making. Here are some techniques to refine your prompts to obtain more precise and useful responses from ChatGPT:

1. Be Specific with Your Request

The specificity of your prompt directly influences the accuracy and relevance of ChatGPT's response. Instead of asking broad questions, pinpoint exactly what you need.

Example:

- Vague: "Tell me about the stock market."

- Specific: "Provide a summary of today's percentage changes for the S&P 500 index and the top three performing sectors."

2. Include Context in Your Prompts

Providing context helps the AI understand the frame of reference and deliver tailored information. Context can be temporal, spatial, or related to particular market conditions.

Example:

- Without Context: "What's the impact of economic indicators on markets?"

- With Context: "What impact do rising unemployment rates in the U.S. typically have on consumer discretionary stocks?"

3. Use Clear and Concise Language

While ChatGPT is adept at processing natural language, clear and concise prompts reduce the chances of misinterpretation and ensure you get straight to the point.

Example:

- Less Clear: "I'm wondering if you could possibly give some insights on, maybe, how tech stocks are doing?"

- Clear and Concise: "What is today's performance of the NASDAQ tech sector?"

4. Sequence Your Questions Logically

When asking multiple questions, structure them logically. This helps ChatGPT provide responses that are coherent and systematically address each part of your inquiry.

Example:

- Logical Sequence:

. *"What was the closing price of XYZ stock today?"*
. *"How does this compare to its price last week?"*
. *"What are the factors driving today's price movement?"*

5. Incorporate Keywords Related to Your Analysis Focus

Using keywords specific to your area of interest, such as particular technical indicators or financial metrics, can guide ChatGPT to focus its response around these concepts.

Example:

- General: *"Can you analyze Apple's stock?"*

- Keyword Specific: *"Can you analyze Apple's stock focusing on its P/E ratio, quarterly earnings growth, and dividend yield for the last quarter?"*

6. Request Summaries for Complex Information

When dealing with complex information, such as lengthy financial reports or market analysis, ask ChatGPT to summarize key points. This can help in quickly grasping essential information.

Example:
Request: *"Summarize the key findings from Apple's 2023 Annual Financial Report."*

7. Clarify Your Desired Level of Detail

Depending on your needs, specify whether you want a detailed analysis or a brief overview. This helps in managing the depth of the response.

Example:

- Brief: *"Give me a quick overview of the current trends in the cryptocurrency market."*

- Detailed: *"Provide a detailed analysis of the current trends in the cryptocurrency market, including the major movers, volume changes, and market sentiment."*

8. Ask for Explanations of Jargon and Complex Concepts

If you're not familiar with specific terms or concepts, ask ChatGPT to explain them. This can enhance your understanding and aid in making more informed decisions.

Example:

Prompt: *"Explain what a 'short squeeze' is and provide recent examples from the stock market."*

By applying these techniques to refine your prompts, you can enhance the quality and applicability of the insights you receive from ChatGPT, making it a more powerful tool in your trading strategy.

Important Note on Handling Fresh Information in Market Queries

When using ChatGPT for trading-related queries, it's crucial to acknowledge the limitations regarding the freshness of information. ChatGPT's training data includes a vast array of sources and historical information up to a certain point in time but does not include real-time updates. This limitation is significant in the trading context where market conditions can change rapidly, and timely information is critical for making informed decisions.

Dealing with the Need for Up-to-Date Information

While ChatGPT provides robust insights based on historical data and learned patterns, for the most current market data or the latest financial news, it may not always have the most up-to-date information. In situations where recent developments are crucial to your trading decisions, I recommend a specific approach:

Use of Direct Search Queries: For obtaining the most current information, consider using real-time search engines or financial news platforms directly. You can enhance your interaction with AI tools that have real-time browsing capabilities by prefacing your prompt with directives like "search on Bing." This method instructs the AI to pull the latest available data from the web, providing you with real-time insights.

Example:

- Standard Prompt: *"What is the latest price of Bitcoin?"*

- Enhanced Prompt for Freshness: *"Search on Bing: What is the latest price of Bitcoin?"*

Tip for Effective Use of Real-Time Data Queries

When you require the latest market data or news updates and are using an AI tool capable of real-time searching, framing your prompts with a directive to search online resources can significantly enhance the relevance and accuracy of the information:

- Be Specific: Clearly define what specific information you need, such as prices, economic indicators, or the impact of recent news on a specific stock or sector.

- Use Keywords: Incorporate relevant keywords that can help in fetching precise information from search engines or databases.

Final Considerations

While AI like ChatGPT offers tremendous advantages in terms of analyzing complex datasets and generating predictive insights based on historical data, for trading decisions that rely on the most current information, always complement AI insights with real-time data obtained directly through live searches or updates from trusted financial news sources. This approach ensures that your trading strategies are both informed by historical data analysis and aligned with the latest market conditions, giving you a well-rounded perspective for making trading decisions.

Continuous Learning

How to use the outcomes of AI-assisted trading decisions to refine further interactions and strategies with ChatGPT.

Using outcomes from AI-assisted trading decisions to refine further interactions and strategies with ChatGPT involves a process of continuous learning and adaptation. This iterative approach not only enhances the precision of your trading strategy but also improves the effectiveness of your communication with ChatGPT. Here's how you can implement this in your trading:

Step 1: Record Outcomes and Feedback

Track Performance:

- Detail Recording: For each trading decision assisted by ChatGPT, record the outcome. This includes the specifics of the advice given, the decisions made based on that advice, and the resulting performance of those decisions.

- Feedback Loop: Create a feedback mechanism where you can evaluate the effectiveness of ChatGPT's advice. Was the information accurate and useful? Did the advice lead to successful outcomes?

Example:

If ChatGPT suggested buying a particular stock based on its volatility and growth potential, note how that stock performed over a set period compared to the market and sector benchmarks.

Step 2: Analyze the Data

Identify Patterns and Anomalies:

- Performance Review: Regularly analyze the tracked data to identify patterns or recurring issues. Are there certain types of advice or specific conditions under which ChatGPT's recommendations tend to succeed or fail?

- Adjustments: Based on your findings, determine if the way you query ChatGPT needs refinement. Perhaps certain phrasing or more specific contexts need to be provided to improve the relevance and accuracy of the responses.

Example:

If you notice that ChatGPT's recommendations on short-term trades consistently underperform, it might indicate a need to adjust how you ask about market timing or to provide it with more detailed current market data.

Step 3: Refine Interactions

Optimize Queries:

- Precision in Asking: Refine how you phrase your questions based on the analysis. If detailed queries yield better results, make sure to incorporate more specifics in your prompts.

- Contextual Updates: As you gather more data, provide ChatGPT with updated contexts and more nuanced information, helping it generate better-tailored advice.

Example:

Instead of asking, "Should I buy tech stocks today?" refine your question to, *"Given the 5% rise in tech sector volatility this week, should I adjust my tech stocks portfolio today?"*

Step 4: Implement Strategic Adjustments

Feedback Implementation:

- Strategy Refinement: Use the insights from your ongoing analysis to adjust your broader trading strategy. This could involve more focused asset allocation, revised risk management tactics, or adjusted entry and exit points.

- Continuous Learning: Implement a continuous learning plan where ChatGPT is regularly updated with new information and feedback on its past performance. This keeps the model relevant and aligned with market changes.

Example:
If analysis shows that ChatGPT performs well in stable markets but not in volatile conditions, you might choose to rely on its advice more during certain market phases and less during others.

Step 5: Scale and Evolve

Expansion of Use Cases:

- Broadening Scope: As you refine your use of ChatGPT, consider expanding the types of trading decisions and analysis where you utilize AI. This can include broader economic analysis, international market trends, or different asset classes.

- Integration with Other Tools: Consider integrating ChatGPT with other AI tools and platforms to enhance your trading system, using ChatGPT for qualitative analysis and other tools for quantitative analysis.

Example:

Combine ChatGPT's insights with quantitative data from algorithmic trading models to develop a hybrid trading strategy that leverages both qualitative insights and quantitative data.

Through this cycle of recording, analyzing, refining, and implementing, you can progressively enhance how you use ChatGPT in your trading activities. This iterative process not only improves your immediate trading outcomes but also evolves your overall trading strategy to be more adaptive and informed by AI-driven insights.

The iterative process of interacting with AI and learning from successes and failures.

Continuous learning in the context of interacting with AI, like ChatGPT, in trading involves an iterative process of dialogue, application, reflection, and adjustment. This process helps traders refine their use of AI over time, learning from both successes and failures to optimize decision-making and improve outcomes. Here's a deeper look into each stage of this iterative process:

1. Dialogue

The initial interaction with AI involves asking questions or seeking advice based on current trading needs. Effective dialogue requires precise and context-rich prompts, as mentioned earlier. The trader must be clear about what information or analysis is needed and provide sufficient detail for the AI to generate relevant and accurate responses.

Example: A trader might ask ChatGPT, *"What are the potential impacts of the upcoming federal interest rate decision on the bond market?"* This specific inquiry sets a focused stage for the AI to provide targeted insights.

2. Application

Once the trader receives advice or analysis from the AI, the next step is to apply this information to actual trading decisions. This could mean executing trades based on the AI's recommendations or adjusting a trading strategy to align with the insights provided.

Example: If ChatGPT predicts that interest rates will likely increase and negatively impact bond prices, the trader might decide to reduce exposure to long-term bonds based on this insight.

3. Reflection

After implementing decisions based on AI interactions, the trader reflects on the outcomes. This reflection should focus on evaluating whether the AI-provided insights were accurate and effective, and how the decisions impacted the trading outcomes. Reflection helps identify what worked well and what did not.

Example: If the trader's decision to sell bonds ahead of the rate hike resulted in a profit or avoided losses, this would be considered a success. If the market reacted differently than expected and the decision led to missed opportunities or losses, this would require further analysis.

4. Adjustment

Based on the reflection phase, the trader makes adjustments to both the approach to interacting with the AI and the trading strategies employed. This might involve changing how questions are phrased, providing different types of information to the AI, or reevaluating the types of trading strategies where AI advice is utilized.

Example: If the trader found that the AI's predictions were frequently off in volatile market conditions, they might adjust by seeking AI input for less volatile conditions or refining the input data used during volatile periods.

5. Feedback Loop

The continuous feedback loop involves regularly updating the AI with new information and outcomes from past advice. This keeps the AI model well-informed and improves its future accuracy and relevance.

Example: Continuously inputting updated market data, outcomes of previous trades influenced by AI advice, and adjustments in market dynamics into ChatGPT helps train the model for better future performance.

6. Scale and Evolve

As confidence in the AI's capabilities grows and as the trader becomes more adept at interacting with the AI, there may be opportunities to scale the use of AI across more types of trading decisions and to integrate other AI tools for more complex analyses.

Example: Expanding AI usage to include international markets analysis, integrating AI-driven quantitative tools, or employing AI for real-time risk assessment.

The iterative process of interacting with AI in trading is a dynamic learning experience that improves over time. By continually dialoguing, applying, reflecting, and adjusting, traders can enhance their strategic approaches and leverage AI more effectively to secure better trading outcomes. This cycle not only improves individual decision-making but also evolves the overall trading strategy to be more adaptive and intelligent.

Conclusion: Leveraging ChatGPT in Trading

Recap of Key Benefits

Using ChatGPT in trading offers several distinct advantages that can significantly enhance a trader's ability to make informed decisions and manage their portfolio more effectively:

1. Enhanced Market Analysis: ChatGPT can quickly digest and summarize vast amounts of financial data and news, providing traders with concise, actionable insights that would otherwise require extensive time to compile.

2. Accessibility to Complex Insights: With its advanced NLP capabilities, ChatGPT democratizes access to complex trading analysis and economic forecasts, which might otherwise be accessible only to professionals with advanced analytical skills.

3. Risk Management: By discussing potential risks and generating scenarios, ChatGPT helps traders identify and mitigate financial risks before they impact portfolios.

4. Efficient Decision Making: ChatGPT can streamline decision-making processes, reducing the time from analysis to action, and enabling traders to respond more quickly to market changes.

5. Continuous Learning and Adaptation: ChatGPT supports an iterative learning process, allowing traders to refine their strategies based on past outcomes and ongoing AI interactions, thereby continually improving their approach.

Encouragement to Explore AI Tools

The landscape of trading is evolving rapidly, with AI technologies at the forefront of this transformation. As such, it is crucial for traders to embrace and integrate these tools into their strategies:

- Stay Curious and Informed: The world of AI is constantly evolving. Staying curious and informed about new developments and technologies can provide a competitive edge. Regularly exploring emerging AI tools and updates to existing platforms like ChatGPT can uncover new opportunities for enhancing trading practices.
- Embrace Experimentation: The best way to understand the potential of AI in trading is through hands-on experience. Traders should experiment with different AI tools to see which ones best complement their trading style and goals. This might include using AI for different aspects of trading, such as predictive analytics, automated trading systems, or sentiment analysis.

- Invest in Learning: The integration of AI requires a fundamental understanding of how these tools work and their implications for trading. Investing time in learning about AI, through courses, webinars, or self-study, can be immensely beneficial. Knowledge empowers traders to use AI more effectively and responsibly.

- Adapt and Innovate: As markets evolve, so too should trading strategies. AI tools like ChatGPT are part of a broader trend towards more data-driven, automated trading environments. Adapting to these changes not only involves adopting new tools but also innovating on how they are applied to remain competitive and profitable.

Quick Win Example with ChatGPT: Optimize Your Trading Portfolio

For a practical and immediate application of ChatGPT in your trading activities, consider this quick win: take a screenshot of your current stock trading portfolio and ask ChatGPT to analyze and suggest optimizations.

Simply upload the screenshot to a platform where ChatGPT is integrated and type, "How can I optimize this portfolio for better performance?" ChatGPT can provide insights on diversification, potential risk areas, and suggest adjustments to enhance your portfolio's overall resilience and growth potential. This direct interaction not only demonstrates ChatGPT's capability in real-time analysis but also offers you actionable recommendations that can be implemented straight away.

Give it a try to see how AI can immediately impact your trading strategy!

Final Thoughts

The integration of AI tools like ChatGPT into trading strategies represents a significant advancement in how traders interact with markets. By leveraging the full spectrum of capabilities offered by AI, traders can enhance their analytical prowess, improve decision-making, and better manage risks. Encouraging a mindset of continuous learning and adaptation will ensure that traders can stay ahead in the ever-evolving trading landscape. Embrace AI, and let it transform your trading journey into one that is more informed, efficient, and adaptive.

Spoiler Alert for Upcoming Book on Revolutionary AI in Trading

As we delve into the world of trading enhanced by Artificial Intelligence, it's clear that no single AI today fully addresses the complex, multifaceted needs of the modern trader. From technical analysis and sentiment analysis to generative models that grasp real-time business developments, the integration of diverse information streams remains a significant challenge.

In my upcoming book, I am excited to introduce an innovative concept: the creation of a new form of AI that synthesizes all these aspects into a single, powerful entity. This new AI, named OPTIMIA, aims to revolutionize how traders interact with market data, sentiment, and technical signals.

OPTIMIA will be uniquely designed to incorporate discussions and exchanges with experienced traders, harnessing not only cutting-edge algorithmic strategies but also the empirical human experience and expertise that only seasoned professionals can provide. This blend of human insight and machine efficiency could set a new standard in trading intelligence.

Additionally, my upcoming book will include transcripts of the dialogues that have contributed to OPTIMIA's refinement. These conversations, held with experienced traders, provide invaluable insights into the iterative development process, showcasing how human expertise and feedback are integral to enhancing OPTIMIA's capabilities. This feature will give readers a unique look at the evolution of AI in trading through real-world interactions.

Stay tuned as OPTIMIA is on its way to transforming the trading landscape by bringing together the best of technology and human experience in one formidable tool. Get ready for a future where AI not only supports but enhances your trading decisions with unprecedented precision and insight.

Epilogue

In the hushed offices of the trading room, where time seemed suspended between figures and curves, Julien contemplated the incessant ballet of transactions. It was a world where money circulated like blood in the veins of a living creature, where every movement, every fluctuation, was a pulse of life. And at the heart of this complex and fascinating world, a new and bewitching presence was making its entrance: Optimia.

Optimia was no mere artificial intelligence. It was a creation of rare beauty, a perfect synthesis of science and art. Its algorithms were as precise as Swiss clocks, but within its code lay an almost human sensibility. It held the promise of the future, that sublime alliance between man and machine.

Julien, an old hand at markets, had always navigated by instinct, guided by an intuition honed over the years. But faced with Optimia, he felt a kind of wonder he hadn't known for a long time. She interpreted data with a clarity and depth that defied comprehension, transforming the mysteries of the marketplace into an ordered symphony.

Their collaboration began like a dance. Optimia, with discreet elegance, offered him advice, predictions. She revealed patterns hidden in fluctuations, trends invisible to the human eye. Julien, reluctant at first, gradually allowed himself to be seduced by this luminous intelligence. Together, they weathered the economic storms, avoiding pitfalls with pinpoint precision, discovering unsuspected treasures in the financial meanders.

Optimia had a grace that transcended mere technology. She was like a modern muse, inspiring Julien to see beyond the numbers, to rediscover the beauty in the workings of the economy. Her predictions weren't just accurate; they were imbued with an understated poetry, a harmony that soothed the torments of uncertainty.

Yet this perfection had a downside. The adrenalin of risk, the exaltation of the unforeseen, faded before the almost divine certainty of Optimia's predictions. Julien found himself nostalgic for those moments of anguish and triumph, when every decision was a risk, every victory a conquest wrested from chaos. He sometimes felt like a navigator whose compass had become too precise, robbing the adventure of its mystery.

But he knew that the future belonged to those who knew how to adapt and evolve. Optimia represented this evolution, a promise of efficiency and prosperity. Together, they were forging a new era, where human and artificial intelligence came together in harmonious symphony. And perhaps, at the end of the road, Julien would rediscover that spark, that passion that had once set his trader's heart aflame.

In the meantime, he savored every moment of this unlikely alliance, this meeting of tradition and innovation, where a new form of greatness was born, a delicate, bewitching melody that resonated in the hushed corridors of the trading room.

Made in the USA
Middletown, DE
23 August 2024

59647150R00071